COLLECTED ESSAYS OF Frederick Bailes

COLLECTED ESSAYS OF Frederick Bailes

DEVORSS & COMPANY
P.O. BOX 550, MARINA DEL REY, CA 90294-0550

ISBN: 0-87516-581-8

Library of Congress Catalog Card No.: 86-71938

Printed in the United States of America

Contents

These essays were originally published
as separate booklets.

Getting What You Go After

FOREWORD

EVERYONE WANTS SOMETHING from life. Not everyone gets what he wants. The tendency then is to assume that those who get good results have some hidden qualities denied the average man—that they possess some mysterious "Divine Spark" that is responsible for their success, and that without this gift it is useless to try to climb.

A golfer with a perfect swing sends the ball straight down the fairway—distance 250 yards. Is it a gift? Not necessarily. That clean rhythmic swing that appears to be one continuous movement is made up of a series of technical adjustments. The beginner who learns each of these steps will develop a swing that brings the same results for him. It is mastery rather than mystery that counts.

I have been fortunate in that my work has thrown me into close contact with great numbers of go-getters. They are corporation executives, writers, directors, actors and actresses, professional men and storekeepers. They range all the way from top-flight poets to world-champion pugilists.

It is noticeable that they are not particularly different from the losers in their native gifts; they differ in their methods and inward attitudes. The loser loses because he uses losing methods; the winner uses winning methods. It is true in life as in golf. Added to this is the fact that even winning methods will fail unless backed up by winning attitudes.

Four principles are dominant in the life of the go-getter. These have been checked and re-checked in tens of thousands of those who get what they go after; they are invariably present. They are woven through the warp and the woof of their thinking. Everyone who ever got what he went after has followed these four steps, either consciously or unconsciously. These principles have always worked for me. I believe they will work for anyone who adopts them as active principles in his business or personal affairs, not merely as theories to talk about.

I am often approached by younger men who ask for a "success formula." There is no such thing. But by learning what a good golfer does the beginner can greatly improve his game, and by finding out the methods employed by those whom we call "go-getters" any person can raise his standard of living and of achievement many notches above what it otherwise would have been.

This booklet should be regarded as a testimonial rather than a preachment. I am fully aware of my own deficiencies; I have made my share of blunders and kicked myself around the office as much as most men have done. But I have discovered some principles that have worked in my favor, and I send them forth with the sincere wish that they might help others to get what they go after.

THE PRINCIPLE OF CLARITY

IN STARTING OUT to get what we go after, the first step is: KNOW CLEARLY WHAT WE WANT.

We must do some clear thinking about the goal. A hunter may scare a dozen ducks up off the water. He would like them all, naturally. But if he fires blindly at "them all" he will probably get none. He must pick out one, get it clearly on his sights, "lead" it accurately, and it is his. The average man has a variety of vague wishes, all desirable. These change from time to time. He must single out the one thing he considers most desirable, and make this the goal. There is always a single-mindedness about the go-getter.

Having selected his object, he must lop off the extraneous matter from it, must make it sharp and distinct. The aims of many are too often hazy and indistinct. Hazy thinking produces hazy acting; clear thinking makes for clear acting. This one goal must be made crystal clear.

For example, one wants "more money." A good aim, but vague. Make it clear. How much more money? I earn $100 a week. Not enough! I want more. "More" is too vague. Just how much more? Set the sights a little higher, say $150 or $200 per week. That's as clear and definite as a bull's-eye. We have the possibility of hitting it. When that is reached the sights can be raised again, as often and as fast as we can go. It is better to do it gradually, because a mental jump from $100 to $500 might be too much at one stride and could result in discouragement, although theoretically it is quite possible to accomplish.

Someone else wants happiness. But happiness is vague. What do we mean by happiness? Don't know exactly! Then we shan't get it. Happiness is not a vague emotion that one just "gets." It is usually tied in with a definite object, such as marriage, the ability to write, to own a nice home, to be appreciated, or to have harmony in one's surroundings. Whatever it is to a particular individual, he must be clear in his own mind about it.

Further, he must gain the inward conviction that it is possible of accomplishment by himself. Many are willing to grant that others may achieve this goal, while scarcely daring to believe that they themselves can have it. In this connection it is well to entertain the belief that when one's desire is born, every channel for its accomplishment is already opened; that the sincere individual will find these channels opening as he applies himself to the succeeding steps.

Write it down. This helps clarify it. One has no idea how hazy his desires are until he sets them down in black and white. A builder would find it difficult to please us if we merely told him we wanted "a house." He demands exact plans and specifications. Builders would find it completely impossible to construct a space vehicle of literally millions of parts, all functioning in perfect interaction, which will take men to the moon and back safely, without the most precise, exact plans and specifications.

There is a deep and often unexplored area in man's thought life, where his desires are fabricated into material form. This creative area will take any idea that is held steadily and clearly enough and will bring it forth in his outer affairs. But he who wishes exact manifestation must furnish exact plans and specifications.

Every successful business organization follows this principle. The automobile industry, for example, plans for a definite amount of business each year. The national and foreign territory is surveyed carefully, and a definite number of possible sales is arrived at. Then a specific quota is assigned to each territory; these cars must be taken. The territorial distributor assigns in turn a definite number to each salesman and expects him to sell them.

This is a specific previewing of a goal and is largely responsible for the phenomenal growth of this industry. Sights are placed on a rifle so that the user can get definite results. He who aims at nothing stands a good chance of hitting it. He who knows clearly what he wants has started into the ranks of the go-getters.

THE PRINCIPLE OF CONCENTRATION

THE SECOND STEP is: GET A SINGLE MIND ON YOUR PLAN.

It has been well said, "To be great, concentrate." Once a person has definitely chosen his goal, he must make that the supreme end of all his efforts. Those who get what they go after are characterized by a peculiar single-mindedness; they make everything contribute to the attainment of the goal. They aim for the bull's-eye every time; they focus and bear down in this direction. Anything that contributes to their chosen end is good; anything that would divert their attention from it is bad. The goal is uppermost in their mind and in their affections.

Sometimes wives have not understood this and have felt that their husbands loved their business more than they loved their wives. The fact is that one must actually have a warm, friendly feeling toward his goal if he is to achieve it. He must think it, dream it, sleep it, eat it.

But he is wise if he does not talk it, for this tends to dissipate the inner energy that is driving him toward his goal. Besides, there is nothing quite so boring as the man who talks of his plans all the time, and the effect upon himself can be disastrous, in that too often a kind of self-hypnosis enters in, and he mistakes his talk of his plans for actual work on the plans.

Man's mind is the most dynamic force in the universe. Any plan held steadily enough is bound to come forth in action. Any thought held unwaveringly has terrific penetrating power.

Take a sunglass; hold it over a sheet of paper, but keep it moving around. Nothing happens. Hold it steadily in one place —it burns through. It's the same sun, the same glass, the same paper. The difference? Concentration. Take the sand on the beach. Let it run idly through your fingers. Feels tickly, that's all. Run it through a sand-blasting hose with a fine nozzle. It will cut every speck of old paint off the car and could cut a hole in the steel itself if held at a direct angle. The difference? Concentration.

Take the wandering, wishing thoughts of the majority. Most persons scatter their thought power in all directions and get nowhere. Here and there one steadily pours his thought force into a single channel and gets what he goes after. The difference? Concentration.

Concentration does not necessarily mean the development of super willpower or taking lessons in holding the mind in one place for long periods of time.

It means what William James called "The expulsive power of a new affection." It calls for a sense of comparative values. One sits alone with himself. He sets the goal on one side, and the many other things he would like to do on the other. He realizes that the one automatically kills off the other. Which does he really want, deep down in his heart? Many say that they want success, and they really imagine they do. But if they choose the lesser aims, or take the easier way, that is what they really want. When it comes to the effort necessary for winning, they shrink back.

We pay the price for what we want, and the price we are willing to pay is the indicator of the value we set upon a thing. Young people often have to face this issue. Many say, "I know I should study, or save some money for my opportunity when it comes. But a fellow has to have recreation." To which we should reply that a fellow does not have to have anything but the thing he really wants. A few hours of dawdling or of transitory pleasure can never bring the deep, substantial satisfaction which comes from getting what you really want in life.

The great majority cling to their pursuit of passing pleasure. We do not blame them, for everyone has a perfect right to decide what he wants and how he is going to go after it. What the go-getters of the world show is a shrewd evaluation of comparative values and the ability to submerge their passing interests in a long-range plan. They have come to see that no happiness is so satisfying as that which comes from a sense of achievement, of "having arrived," of the sense of security which grows out of having made a place for themselves.

Still, there are millions who lack the foresight and the sturdiness of character to measure future happiness against passing pleasure. They have no sense of comparative values. And in later life, pushed aside by a hard, practical world that demands results, they whine, "I never had a chance." They forget that no one ever had a chance except the one who was willing to pay the price for it. Mankind seems always to be faced with the necessity of denying itself pleasures now or necessities later on. Willingly now, or unwillingly later on. A well-balanced mind is shown by its ability to place proper values on proper objects.

There are really only two classes of persons in the world—the winners and the whiners. They are spelled with just one letter different, but they are poles apart regarding the difference between their views of life. The winner never whines, and the whiner never wins.

When it comes to charting one's course, or when things go wrong, the whiner always looks outside of himself for the cause of his grief. He is never to blame. It is never his fault. If he had had a different environment, or a different wife, or a better sales territory, or if the boss had only given him some good breaks, he would have done all right.

On the contrary, the person who is of the stuff of which winners are made backs himself up against a wall when things go wrong and looks within himself for the cause of his misfortune. Then, determined to correct his own mental attitudes, he does not ask for "the breaks." All he asks for is an opportunity to get in some hard licks on anything like even terms—in fact, on any terms, for success comes from inside a man. The history of our leading men is largely that of men who saw a goal, took off their coats, and pitched in. But they had a sense of comparative values and knew what was most worth while. This is what we mean by concentration.

Concentration involves self-denial. Branches must be pruned from a tree if one wants bigger and better fruit. The athlete submits himself to rigid discipline, denies himself the passing pleasure of indulgence, while in training. His friends pity him as he goes to bed just as they start out for an evening's pleasure. But it is the price he must be willing to pay to get to the top. Often he is tempted to take the easy way, but his good judgment reasserts itself, and he comes back to his evaluation of comparative values even if he pities himself a little now and then. But ask him, as he gains the championship, if it was worth it. Never mind the answer—that grin tells the story.

Some people imagine that they are hopelessly handicapped because they did not get a college education. Yet anyone can walk into the public library and find books that will give him the equivalent of a college education. Let him select a subject —any subject that seems in line with his goal. It may be coal, carpentering, or chemistry. He can take the simplest book on the subject; the librarian will even help him find the proper books. Twenty-five cents' worth of pencil and paper will give him a hundred dollars' worth of information. "But I don't know how to take notes." Neither does anyone else until he starts. Just write down anything that interests you as you go along. Like an athlete in training, go there every night. I defy anyone, no matter how limited he may think himself mentally, to spend his evenings in this way for three months without being worth more wages. If his own employer does not recognize it, he can sell his greater knowledge to some other employer.

"But when would I go to a show, or a dance?" If that is the reaction after reading this far, it might be better to stop reading right here and ask the bookseller for a refund, because this book is evidently not for you.

Concentration upon a goal makes one's mind alive to that thing, for the channels of one's innermost self are now opening up to it. A chance conversation often uncovers a valuable idea, because seemingly unrelated things fly to and cluster around it. This is one of the rewards of getting a single-minded interest in something. A line in a newspaper, a word on the air, a window display—anything is likely to stir up a new train of thought along this particular line, things that we would have missed entirely otherwise, for when the mind is uncentered these contributory sources never reach the active brain centers.

Concentration affects the whole man, even to his friendships. He concentrates his friendships, keeping them as much as possible to the go-getter type. This does not mean that he becomes a social climber or that he "tags on" to the rich. It simply means that he is wiser to mingle with people who have ideas above those of the wandering crowd. Mix with lazy, unambitious persons and the tendency is to become as they are. Mingle with those who have ideas of getting somewhere, for this keeps the mental attitudes in the direction of expansion instead of contraction and keeps the thought life concentrated along the same lines as the life of outward effort.

"Birds of a feather flock together." This is far more true of the thought patterns than of the physical mingling.

People usually shun the company of someone who they think has a contagious disease, for they do not like contamination. Yet far more deadly is the influence of the whiner, the defeated person, who is sure the world is against him, who lifts his dulled eyes to heaven and says, "Life is not fair. There are no opportunities today." Forget it, and forget him. The world is alive and shrieking with opportunity to the person who is alive.

THE PRINCIPLE OF DECISION

THE THIRD STEP is: MAKE YOUR OWN DECISIONS: STAND ON YOUR OWN TWO FEET.

Decisiveness is the mark of a clean-cut character. Wobbly-mindedness is fatal to success. The Good Book says, "He that wavereth is like a wave of the sea driven by the wind and tossed. Let not that man think that he shall receive anything." The go-getter may not be a blustering, noisy person; in fact he is often the quietest of men, but he does not allow other people to make his decisions for him. He knows how to make up his mind.

There is a common tendency in human nature to assume that the successful man has access to some secret store of wisdom closed to ordinary mortals; that he has some mysterious formula for arriving at truth. The fact is that he has learned to rely upon his own judgment by relying upon it. This is the only secret. There is no magic path to decision of character. It is often developed by hard and painful experience.

He who is always asking advice on his problems will never develop sturdy, self-sufficient decisiveness. Far better for him to make his own decisions, even though many of them are wrong, than to be always right through following the judgment of others. Every choice that he makes, good or bad, brings him nearer to the mature, balanced judgment he wishes to develop. John Wanamaker built such a successful business that people thought he had unerring judgment. He said of himself that he made many incorrect decisions; that if he made 51 correct decisions out of 100 he succeeded; if he made only 49 he would be a failure. Many other go-getters have made similar remarks.

The only way to arrive at a correct conclusion is to get the facts. The vice-president of a vast corporation, who made decisions of great importance very quickly, told me that when he started as a young man he was advised to get all the facts and set them down on two sheets of paper, one for and one against. On one sheet he set down all the reasons for deciding one way; on the other, all the reasons for the opposite choice. Then he went very carefully down the two lists to learn which side had weightier facts. When he found one argument in the "Yes" column which offset one in the ''No'' column he scratched off the ''No'' argument, and vice versa. In this way he eliminated many of them on both sides, finally arriving at a few strong reasons on either side. Finally one set outweighed the other. There was his decision.

One who does this will find his courage growing, his confidence in his own judgment increasing, his self-reliance and decisiveness becoming more prominent, and his judgment more accurate. After a while, paper will become unnecessary. It can be done swiftly in the mind.

Another thing that the go-getter stresses is that it is a bad thing to reconsider that decision. The human mind has a curious way of doubting itself. After a decision, the beaten arguments set up a clamor, for many of them were valid arguments. Reconsidering them makes for wobbly-mindedness. Tell them, ''Yes, I know that all you say is true, but you were outweighed by the facts on the other side. You are good, but I have decided in favor of the better. Now get out of here. I have work to do.'' Then turn your attention to the next thing.

Decisiveness is often shown, as well as developed, by refusing to do certain things for others. The question of how much assistance to give others is one of the most difficult to decide. The average person does not wish to be selfish, but this often leads him into doing things for others to such an extent that he wrongs them in the long run.

No one likes to turn a deaf ear to another in distress. But some persons, without knowing it, become parasites, always wanting help. They possess an uncanny ability to get into tight spots where the situation is desperate and immediate aid is required. No one wishes to appear hard-hearted; therefore aid is given repeatedly. Yet the judgment shows that no permanent good is done; and while the reason warns against giving further help, the heart gives in and the helping hand is extended. Therefore it has become an axiom with successful people: "Never do too much for others, even the members of one's own family."

While it is true that a little assistance rendered at a crucial moment has often meant the difference between success and failure to someone, it is likewise a fundamental fact of human experience that "every tub must stand on its own bottom." Human nature shrinks from standing on its own feet; there is always a tendency to lean on someone else where possible; but life has always advanced through those persons who single-handedly faced and solved their problems, often with much inward trepidation.

Courage grows by use, just as one's judgment does. After a few experiences of solving his own problems the individual finds that he possesses much more sturdiness of character than he had thought and is on his way to becoming a go-getter. Through constant help extended to those who should be helping themselves, we harm them by stunting their growth and leave them weaker than we found them.

I recall a boyhood experience. Ten eggs were set under a hen. Nine hatched on time, but one chick kept tapping inside the egg for two days longer, unable to break through its shell. I ran to my father for permission to help the chicken out, and my father's seemingly cruel reply is as true of people as of chickens. It was, "No, son, a chicken that is not strong enough to break its own shell is not strong enough to be worth much when you break the shell for it."

Decision of character is often shown more by our refusals than our grants because they are much more difficult to make.

Gratitude is not an outstanding feature of the human race. Some persons will draw repeatedly upon one for years, and when finally they are refused aid, they will turn against the donor with bitterest venom. By a strange psychological trait, men come to hate those who do too much for them and love those for whom they sacrifice. Men at the top have often said, "My bitterest enemies are those whom I have helped most; it makes me hesitate about helping anyone."

Decision of character is shown by the power to initiate new activities. Some people are always "going to" do something, always have plans. But conditions are never just right for them to start. They go through life in a timid flutter of procrastination, or in the warm, drugged glow of castles in the air, under which they never seem to get the foundations laid. They dream dreams and make plans. But they never get started, for they are in a state of self-hypnosis.

Our procrastinations may be the result of unrecognized fear, and our arguments are what the psychologist calls rationalization; that is, we are afraid to face the task so we bring up arguments that keep us from feeling that we are dodging the issue. We are filled with a holy zeal for the thing we are "going to" do some day, and we wallow in the nice feeling. But that is as far as we get.

Why don't we start? Well, you see, it's this way. This is election year, or a depression is on or may be just around the corner, or I'll wait until the children are bigger, or until certain obstacles are out of the way. The real reason is that we are afraid to start.

If fear is at the root of our hesitation, then months or years from now, when it is not election year, and the depression is over, the children grown and every other obstacle removed, we shall find a brand-new crop of obstacles blocking our way, because the obstacles are never out in the world but deep within the heart. The person who can master himself can master the world. And does!

THE PRINCIPLE OF TENACITY

THE FOURTH STEP is: KEEP YOUR FACE TOWARD THE GOAL.

Hang on like a bulldog. The road to achievement is seldom straight and smooth. It is much more likely to be a series of ups and downs. The person doesn't live whose life has been one long string of unbroken victories. Many of today's most successful corporations have had bitter experience of receiverships in the past. William Wrigley was forced to quit three times, broke. But he never quit inside; he went on to get what he went after.

When Abraham Lincoln was a young man he ran for the legislature and was badly swamped. He next entered business, failed, and spent seventeen years paying up the debts of a worthless partner. He fell in love with a beautiful woman, to whom he became engaged—she died. He ran for Congress—was badly defeated. He tried to get an appointment to the U.S. Land Office—was turned down. He became candidate for the U.S. Senate—was badly defeated. In 1856, as candidate for the Vice-Presidency, same result. In 1858 he was defeated by Douglas.

But in the face of repeated defeat and apparent failure he eventually achieved the highest success possible to an American and undying fame.

The whiner stays down after a few blows, and the world thereafter has to listen to his wails. The winner gets up again and again. The person who refuses to stay down can't be licked. Times come when one wonders if the prize is worth the pounding he is taking, and he is tempted to quit.

Never quit under fire or when the tide is running against you. The person who does this loses his tempered fineness and becomes base iron. The world may say you are through.

Your friends may say the same. But no one is beaten until he himself lies down. As long as one gets up and struggles in the general direction of the goal, he is winning, whether he looks like a winner or not. He may not be making as rapid progress as he would like, but as long as he keeps his eye on the goal, he is winning.

It is twenty-two miles from England to France, but swimmers know that they will be compelled to swim almost twice that to get across. They are carried off a straight course by crosscurrents. At times they are actually being carried away from the shore they are trying to reach, but they know there is no other way to get across. So they settle down to the grind, face the punishment and bafflement they are forced to take, knowing that they are winning as long as they keep going in the general direction, no matter where temporary currents may carry them.

So keep going when the going is hardest. People with the finest chances of success often quit when another day's stick-to-itiveness would have brought them to their goal. The channel swimmer knows that the tide can't run out all the time. It has to change. Your "streak of hard luck" can't run forever. It has to change, and perhaps very suddenly.

So fight grimly on, and when you can no longer fight, hang on, refusing to go down. At this stage all the silent forces in the universe begin to pull for you, where before they seemed to be pushing against you. Mentally you tune in with all the fighters of the ages and begin to draw new strength from them.

Let us imagine some hard-hitting businessman in New York is using all his courage, skill, and ingenuity to stay with a deal and close it. All that courage is going out into the universe for other fighters to share. The minds of all go-getters vibrate on the same wave length. They pass on their courage and strength to one another. As all receiving sets throughout the country are tied together by invisible radio waves, so are the minds of men united by invisible thought waves. Thus the man on the Pacific Coast who refuses to quit automatically tunes in with the man in New York who is winning his battle and draws strength from him.

The fraternity of bulldogs is the noblest on earth. Tied together by invisible currents of thought stronger than steel bands, they draw upon one another, although they may never meet in the flesh. They get what they go after, not because they have greater gift, education, or pull than others, but because they have the tenacity to hang on when the going becomes tough, until they eventually wear out the demons of discouragement. They exchange the yellow streak for the red badge of courage.

Healing the "Incurable"

THE TITLE OF THIS essay might appear to be anomalous, for if something is incurable, the question of its healing is immediately wiped out, and there would be no purpose in discussing it. At the outset, therefore, it is well to define "incurability." The term is used in the common acceptation as used by a doctor. Certain conditions are called curable, others incurable. Again, a condition which at its inception may be accounted curable may progress to the point where the amount of tissue destroyed causes it to be classed as incurable. This is the judgment of human wisdom after surveying the resources of the doctor and the history of similar cases.

The Science of Mind recognizes a Healing Principle in the universe; this Principle is evidently far more potent than human effort; its effects have been observed by physician and layman in numerous instances where the patient has recovered after having been given up to die. Therefore we start with the emphatic statement that THERE ARE NO INCURABLE DISEASES. The literature of spiritual healing is replete with instances of the healing of the most serious maladies. In explanation the doctor says, "Nature"; the spiritual healer says, "Healing Principle" or "God."

Diseases which were listed as incurable thirty years ago are now curable by the doctor. They were no more incurable then than now. The "wonder drugs" to cope with them were simply not available then. The absence of cure was due to the absence of professional knowledge. Malignant tumors classed as incurable today will be pronounced completely curable by the doctor in, we hope, the not-too-distant future, as scientists continue their research into this malady; therefore, "curability" and "incurability" are relative terms denoting scientific ability to understand and cope with physical conditions which in themselves are not incurable.

WHAT DOES THE HEALING?

HUMBLE PHYSICIANS HAVE always said that they administered drugs but that God healed. Men have recognized the presence of a Super-Intelligence, which evidently laid hold on the drugs and used them in the restoration of the body. In the instances in which healing occurred without medication, it is evident that this Intelligence was able to effect the restoration without the drug. While we may be unable to offer a satisfactory explanation of what went on, we must admit that something happened, for the patient recovered. Quite evidently there was intelligent activity, for nothing occurs in the universe without intelligence. Later, we hope to trace what appears to have gone on.

TREATMENT FOR PARALYSIS

HERE IS AN example. A man came to a spiritual practitioner, his leg and arm on one side of the body paralyzed. He knew little if anything of the principles of spiritual healing, but he believed something could be done because he had seen a friend healed years ago.

The practitioner spoke to him in some such words as these: "Scientists tell us that there is enough power locked up in a drop of water to run all the wheels in a factory if it could be released. They have unlocked terrific power from certain tiny atoms already. Your body is largely water; therefore right now in your leg and arm is all the power needed to move them freely. The trouble is not absence of power but stoppage of power." The interview lasted for at least an hour, the man showing high intelligence by the type of questions he asked.

The practitioner then gave him treatment, the core of which was that there was no one nor anything in the universe which wished to keep him lame or to interfere with his free locomotion; that his body had been constructed to move easily and freely; therefore this condition was foreign to the intelligent plan for his body; that there was nothing buried deep within his own thought which unconsciously clung to his infirmity, nor was there any sense of guilt which unconsciously made him feel that this was a punishment; that the One Intelligence which built his body in the first place understood fully how to build right action again; that Power and Intelligence are one and the same thing in different manifestations, and that the Intelligence that could lock Itself within an atom could as easily release Itself when there was no longer anything in this man's mind which denied the truth of the words being spoken. Then the man was released mentally to the Intelligence and went home.

An hour or so later, his wife telephoned to say that he had got out of the car unaided for the first time in years. The following week, he was grasping things with his previously paralyzed fingers, and the improvement has continued.

"MIRACLES"

SO-CALLED MIRACLES are never the violation of law. They are merely the introduction of some hitherto unknown or little-used law whose operation is on a higher plane than those with which we have previously worked. Man has kept himself in prison because he has looked backward. He has believed that conditions ineffectually treated before must of necessity continue to defy man's efforts to dislodge them. Man must learn to look forward toward the discovery of other laws which supersede the imprisoning laws.

Fifty years ago, most persons would have jeered at the man who said that one could sing into a microphone and be heard instantly around the world, or that the images of actors could be passed through walls and doors to be seen, as in life, miles away on a television screen. They might even have said that these things were against the laws of nature. Yet man's every advance from primitive to modern has come from his coming to understand and use higher law than the previous generation knew.

Man has explored the distant corners of the earth's surface; he has drilled miles beneath; he has captured secrets of the sunspots and has made himself well acquainted with the invisible rays that pierce his body momentarily. But he has been late in exploring his own mind and the deeper Intelligence of the Infinite.

Now he is awakening to the fact that there are invisible

rays of a spiritual nature, hitherto largely untapped except by men like Jesus and other spiritual healers. Some of the outstanding physicists are openly proclaiming that the next great search beyond radar will be the quest for a pulsation believed to exist, compared to which radar is gross and earthy. They believe this to be possessed of tremendous healing force, operating through and registered by the spiritual nature of man, which will unlock for man a glorious future of health and well-being. Thus the metaphysics of today becomes the physics of tomorrow.

THE RELATION OF FAITH TO HEALING

WE VENTURE A prediction. It is that if laboratory research succeeds in isolating these spiritual pulsations, it will be found that they operate only through those who are attuned to spiritual impulses, and that "a humble and a contrite heart" is their vehicle. What is now called faith will then be seen as a consciousness attuned to spiritual Reality, and the emphasis upon faith as a requirement for healing, advanced by scientists like Carrel and metaphysicians like Jesus, will be understood. It will be found that hate is the static that interferes with their reception and that love smooths them in, that fear "jams" them and that quietness lets them through. The emphasis upon peace, love, and brotherhood found in all the ancient sacred books, which have been spurned as impractical in the world's frantic rush for baubles, will be found always to have been not only up to date but ahead of the times. Spiritual knowledge blazes the way; physical knowledge gropes its faltering way later (then claims the discovery).

The Science of Mind is a philosophy that is based upon reason as well as faith; so it reaches out eagerly for any new discovery by the scientific world. The amazing thing is that every new discovery helps substantiate the postulates of spiritual healing. Science is becoming more spiritual and the church must become more scientific, for the Infinite Intelligence is a Spiritual Thinker operating scientifically in the universe, therefore equally the Author of spiritual and material science.

"Incurability" is a relative term. That which is incurable to a child is not so to an adult. A child would find it impossible to lift a motorcycle up onto its two wheels; a man finds it possible. The difference lies in the resources which each has to bring to bear. Thus the statement "With God all things are possible" is not so foolish as it might appear.

I visited a friend. His dog was tied outside to a tree. Going out afterwards, I found the dog had circled the tree until there were only a few inches of free rope. He was miserable, hopeless, "incurable," his head held down at an awkward angle.

A greater intelligence could take him as I did, lead him back several times and free him. To him this might be a miracle. It was merely a higher application of law. He had used law to bind himself. I used the same law to free him. The same law that brings illness will heal us when we reverse our thought. There are no incurable diseases, only incurable ways of approaching them.

WHO AND WHAT IS GOD?

MANY PERSONS ARE repelled by the word "God." This is understandable because their childhood associations with the word were fearsome or silly or the word was mouthed by hypocrites. But the word is a good one and mature persons need not shrink from it. It is only a term used by man to express that which all men instinctively feel exists. No other term is so comprehensive. The words "Mind," "Intelligence," "Law," "Order," "Harmony," the "Infinite," "Nature" all leave something to be desired, while "God" is a short word including all these phases. When used in these writings it has no sanctimonious connotation; it applies to the pervading Intelligence which operates in order and in love, which is indefinable and which cannot be described or fully analyzed.

It is evident that man knows very little of the nature of God; yet close observation leads us to believe that this Super-Intelligence is characterized by an "All-ness" on three sides. This lays the foundation for a reasonable working hypothesis upon which to base our belief that all disease is curable.

OMNISCIENCE

THE FIRST IS Omniscience, or All-Knowledge. It is apparent that God possesses knowledge necessary to create anything. This knowledge must be the source of all man's knowledge. Man's understanding and use of geometric patterns is matched to the smallest detail in the circles, triangles, cubes, parallelograms, and other geometrical figures found in the minute structure of cells, crystals, and other minutiae of creation. In fact, what man calls his knowledge is in reality only his finding out a Super-Knowledge which has existed from all time. The highest pinnacle of learning to which man will eventually come has all been known from eternity by Super-Intelligence. This Intelligence built a universe, a man, a cell easily and effortlessly. Quite evidently It knows how to rebuild any part in what we call healing. Man's twentieth-century knowledge is as a drop in the ocean to Omniscience.

The boy is proud when he takes a watch to pieces. The higher intelligence that designed the various watch parts, constructed them, assembled them into an accurate measurer of time is necessary to rebuild and repair that watch.

Man is justly proud of his discovery of the structure of the atom, but Omniscience originated the design, knowing exactly how many electrons were necessary to circle the nucleus in order for it to be an atom of uranium, and how many for it to be an atom of helium. It has the knowledge of the way to build this frozen force into solid structure, to make it cohere, to assemble it into gigantic structures which circle in space at exact distances, perpetually in order and in time.

Man can imitate a blade of grass, but he cannot make one that will grow, for Omniscience still possesses the guarded secret of Life which man hopes one day to uncover.

The scientist is the boy taking the watch to pieces; Omniscience is the watch builder, which appears quite willing to build anew when certain conditions are met.

What is the power which holds our weighty planet in place, ceaselessly spinning and circling on its elliptical path through space, on a course as unvarying as though it were fastened to a railroad track? The scientist talks vaguely of "gravitational pull" and "time-space," not knowing what either of these is. When the secret is eventually discovered, it will be found that this tremendous power so effortlessly exerted is merely Thought, the product of Intelligence. The ultimate discovery will probably be that Thought and Power are the same thing, or two phases of the same thing.

Omniscience knows what to do with the seed dropped into

the earth, surrounding it with the particular type of environment friendly to it, so that it can draw upon this environment. Yet further thought tells us that the seed has no power to draw, for it has no inherent intelligence. Omniscience draws through it.

Anyone can place seeds in the ground and *let* them grow, but a man would be fully occupied *making* one seed grow, supervising the complex chemical activities necessary to life. To do it for one hundred or one thousand seeds would drive the best human being crazy; yet without the slightest effort Omniscience supervises a billion seeds. This is the Wisdom with which we deal in spiritual healing.

There is no problem anywhere, no matter how great, that Omniscience cannot solve. Due credit should be given for the skill of the physician, but his highest knowledge is but an infinitesimal percentage of All-Knowledge. Omniscience is not 99%; it is 100%. It is ALL the knowledge there is or ever will be. It is not derogatory of the physician to say that man must free himself from a slavish fatalistic belief that anything is incurable just because a physician in whom he has great confidence says so. It probably is incurable from the standpoint of partial knowledge, but not from that of Total Knowledge.

Omniscience extends not only to the farthest reaches of trans-stellar space; it works intimately within the tiniest point of the human body. It took a fertilized ovum and out of its stores of knowledge built each minute particle of a complicated machine and brought it out into the world, a living soul equipped to meet and grapple with life. Since it had the necessary knowledge to build a body out of the common materials circulating in the mother's blood, it certainly has not forgotten how new cells are built. Sometimes it amazes humanity by doing some remarkable rebuilding without human intervention after man has done his best and failed. Usually the prerequisite is a human consciousness that says, "I believe that ALL the wisdom of God is rebuilding this body now."

OMNIPOTENCE

THE SECOND PHASE is Omnipotence, All-Power. Not alone the knowledge but the power to transmute that knowledge into new tissue. A theory may be beautiful but it is useless unless it works. A movement grows only by the results it produces. In our Sunday morning lectures, there have been reported over and over healings of malignant growths, heart conditions, ulcers, arthritis, and other conditions, once there was borne in upon the consciousness an awareness of Omnipotence—of a Power before which this seemingly intractable condition is nothing.

A person may bring himself to regard a serious growth as of no more moment than a pimple. People know that pimples disappear after a short time. As a result they do not fear them, knowing they are not dangerous. They know vaguely that there is some chemical action or some power which automatically seems to remove them. When they are able to lift their awareness of this Power to the point where even the serious condition is seen to be as no more than a pimple to the Power, they are fulfilling another condition of healing. It might be stated in this way: As long as the fear of the condition outweighs the knowledge of the Power, there is no healing; as soon as the knowledge of the Power outweighs the fear of the condition, healing occurs.

Many "little" things are healed with a partial consciousness and a weak faith, but from time to time conditions arise which call for not some but all of the Power of God, hence the need for a consciousness of Omnipotence, in which all man's puny fears can be immersed forever.

OMNIPRESENCE

THE THIRD FACTOR entering into healing the "incurable" is Omnipresence, this Power everywhere present. Man's thinking is so bound by human senses that the idea of Omnipresence is not always easy to grasp. He is accustomed to think of God as localized. If a man is at one spot, he cannot simultaneously be at a different spot unless he is divided into two parts. If a thing is divided, each part becomes weaker. But the Infinite is not divisible, therefore is not localized. All of God is present at any point where any of God is. Since man has observed the Super-Intelligence way out in space and at the same time buried in the infinitesimal atom, he knows that a characteristic of God must be Omnipresence.

The significance of this in healing has been overlooked. Man can readily grasp the concept of God as filling distant space; he can carry this over into a belief that Super-Intelligence fills the atmosphere about his city, for he sees the stars above; he can make it more intimate by imagining that it fills the room in which he is, that it permeates his clothing; then he can make it intensely personal by thinking of it as saturating his hair, his skin, penetrating within to the most central cell of his body. In this latter he is supported by the physiologist who sees the working of Intelligence in the chemistry of the single cell. He calls it Intelligence; we call it the Infinite Healing Presence. Does the terminology matter? Does it matter if we call it Nature or God?

What does matter is the way in which we see it. Not what man sees but its implications are what count. A physician and a carpenter will observe the human chest breathing. The latter will see the chest rise and fall; that is all. The former immediately has a picture of nerve impulses which initiate an arching movement in a curved thin muscle called the diaphragm; he will mentally see the sliding of the pleural membranes over one another as the breath is inhaled and expelled; he may visualize valvular action in the pulmonary artery and an interchange of carbon dioxide and oxygen in the lung, or he may think of the important work of the bronchi at this stage. The carpenter sees a mechanical movement; the physician sees a life process, a mystery of Intelligence.

In like manner, one may intellectually agree on the fact of Omnipresence but miss its implications. It is not enough to believe it; one must get the vital awareness of it. He must know that it is the nature of this Intelligence to heal, to work always toward the normalizing of things. He must know that just as the naval architect builds into his ship a desire and an ability to fight back onto an even keel after being laid over on its side, so this Intelligence built into man's body the same ability to come back onto an even keel.

More than this, he must recognize that man did not invent this desire, but that it is quite evidently the desire and intention of the Divine Architect; therefore he sees not merely an impersonal Intelligence operating through physical law as the physiologist sees, carrying on the complex processes of nutrition, elimination, and cell division; he sees something much closer and warmer, a Personal Physician, intensely interested in restoring balance ruined by man's ignorance of the delicate equilibrium of cells. This broadening of implications means the difference between intellectual assent and saving faith.

But there is a further reason for a living acceptance of the fact of Omnipresence. Whenever or wherever distress is, it is an evidence that we have surrendered our belief in Omnipresence at this point. This Intelligence is perfect in its working, peaceful in its effect, healthy in its manifestation, for health is natural while illness is unnatural. To the degree that one is conscious of disease, he is practicing nonbelief in Omnipresence. Either God is present at every tiny point, or God is not Omnipresent.

In one sense our surrender to illness is a denial of Omnipresence. We assist in our healing when we declare, "Right where that trouble seems to be, God is, as the Infinite Healing Omnipresence. Not near, not all around, but right in the middle of it, filling that spot to the limit so that there is no room for anything unlike Itself. I surrender myself, thought and body, to the flow of Omnipresence."

ALL-KNOWLEDGE AND ALL-POWER EVERYWHERE PRESENT

ALL-KNOWLEDGE AND All-Power at All-points. A general deploying his forces must weaken one point in order to take some men from it to attack at another point. He cannot throw his full strength at more than one point simultaneously. Man tends to carry over this human concept when considering the Infinite. But the word "Infinite" is not easily understood by humans. We have the feeling that Divine Intelligence must have other interests besides ours; therefore there must be a diminution in the Power available for us. What we must come to grasp is that all the undivided attention of Super-Intelligence is concentrated on our problem, as though there were not another person in the universe, nor a blade of grass nor a star. One of the secrets of Jesus' power was that he considered himself the only-begotten Son of the Father; hence it was easy to feel that all the Father's resources were at his disposal.

Better still, each person can hold this idea of the power of God in its entirety for him, without any of them having any the less. The Inexhaustible cannot be exhausted; the Undepletable can never be depleted; therefore man can draw upon reserves of Power which are eternally maintained.

USING THESE RESOURCES

THE QUESTION WHICH might arise is, "How are we to draw upon these Infinite resources?"

First of all, there is no "Gift of Healing" bestowed upon particular individuals. The same law is available to all men, rich, poor, ignorant, educated, famous, unknown. There must be a surrender of one's fears and human estimates, losing them in the sense of the Allness of God. In *Your Mind Can Heal You*, I have gone more fully into the exact methods to be followed, but a simple thing to remember is that there is no tissue dense enough to shut out the fine spiritual vibrations of Omnipresence.

Agnes Sanford, in an excellent book, *The Healing Light*, relates an incident which is simple in its procedure, yet powerful in its effect. She tells that her child was ill for six weeks with suppurated ears. She had prayed earnestly, and as a minister's wife she knew the power of prayer, but was bitterly disappointed as her child continued to suffer. A ministerial friend dropped in and, hearing of the trouble, went upstairs to pray for the child. His prayer was simple: "O God, we ask You to send Your Life into this baby's ears and make them well. We thank You because we know this is being done. Amen."

The baby slept and from that day on has had no recurrence of the trouble.

We cite this instance as an encouragement to others, for it is Godlike in its simplicity and may become the starting point for others. Further on, Mrs. Sanford recommends saying "Thank You" much oftener than "Please." When we are thankful before the answer comes, it is an indication that we believe the work has already been done. This is the highest form of faith.

Healing comes by a recognition of the fact that the Power that built the body did not immediately lose all interest in it. It has as much interest now as when it carefully built and assembled it cell by cell. But man has been falsely taught that sickness is God's punishment for sin, when the truth is that it is the punishment BY sin; when man turns from the sin of his murky, earth-blinded attitudes and beliefs, he finds the Infinite Healing Presence waiting, ready to sweep in as automatically as air sweeps into a vacuum. "The Lord thy God is in the midst of thee, mighty to save."

The Secret of Healing

THERE IS NO SECRET of healing, for its method is spread across the face of nature. Starting less than one hundred years ago, the mental-spiritual healing movement has spread, slowly at first, but with accelerated pace during the past two or three decades. It was not a new movement, for throughout history there have been fully authenticated healings of this nature. But they were widely separated in time and place, sometimes a whole century elapsing between them. Jesus was one of the few to attract widespread attention by this method of healing; the others get only passing mention.

In the past century, however, the movement has grown by leaps and bounds. The "converts" have been gathered into various organizations, the literature of healing has been multiplying, and even the medical profession, attracted by the unmistakable results, has started to investigate the laws by which these healings have been brought about. As a result, it has added courses in psychosomatic medicine to the curricula of various medical schools.

REASON FOR INCREASE OF MENTAL-SPIRITUAL HEALING

THIS MOVEMENT HAS grown by the fact that it has produced definite and incontrovertible results. Treated at first with scorn by those steeped in the old idea that a physical body needed "something stronger than thought" to heal it, it has made its way through its demonstrations. Those who had seen friends and relatives, given up as hopeless by the doctor, restored to joyous health and vitality through mental-spiritual treatment were thus compelled by the evidence of their own senses to admit that a definite "something" had taken place. Thus the circle was gradually widened, and a broader fringe was thrown out beyond the circle of those healed. This led in turn to a still wider circle. Thus the truth has grown.

ATTITUDES TOWARD MEDICAL ASSISTANCE

SOME DYED-IN-THE-WOOL spiritual practitioners do not permit those they treat to use medical assistance. We do not take this extreme attitude; we know that medicinal assistance has often had a very beneficial effect. But at the beginning of the modern movement the leaders broke clean and said: "Not one drop of medicine" and "Doctors cause more disease than they cure." The practice of medicine at that time was extremely crude; many doctors were ignorant men who had learned their profession by extreme shortcuts, and the stock-in-trade of some of them was a bag of leeches and a supply of calomel. So the patients were perhaps delivered from a worse fate by turning to spiritual healing.

Medical practice in this day has advanced its knowledge considerably and refined its practice. Moreover, it is adding a certain amount of the mental approach, which we trust will increase. We feel therefore that the person who wishes to have medical assistance is quite within his rights; however, since the profession admits that the majority of its patients' troubles originate in their tangled emotions, we stress the necessity of the healing from the inside out.

The dyed-in-the-wool attitude had one serious drawback. Sometimes the person being treated was allowed to sink constantly lower, showing that either his or his practitioner's consciousness was not clear enough to accomplish the healing. Some passed on, when it might have been that the broader view, furnishing them with some material assistance, would have brought them recovery by removing some physical obstruction or rectifying conditions which were plainly the effect of violation of natural law.

We do not criticize the individual who either takes or refrains from medicine, because we believe that this is a matter for the individual consciousness. Some persons have such a high consciousness that drugs would not affect them beneficially anyway, for they are above drugs. If so, medical treatment would only harm them.

THE ART OF HEALING

Mental Healing has called for a decided departure from the views of healing treatment held up until this time in that it has shifted the origin of disease and of health from the body to the mind and emotions.

Moreover, the knowledge and understanding of the techniques involved have been greatly increased by the continuity of the movement. Whereas in olden times one healer worked by himself and left no notes on his methods, the modern exponents of spiritual healing build from generation to generation on the written material left by their predecessors. Thus, there is improvement and advancement of techniques, and the gradual accumulation of a vast body of factual material which is being scanned, dissected, and analyzed by earnest and capable students, who build upon it "more stately mansions."

The procedure at the present might be called an art rather than a science, judged by twentieth-century standards of material science, for its practitioners are not required to study modern bacteriology, embryology, endocrinology, or even the older sciences of anatomy and physiology, in order to practice it; therefore, when he approaches his work, the practitioner does not have the kind of scholastic background which is usually considered scientific, although some practitioners are fortunate enough to have this.

THE SCIENTIFIC ASPECT

The practitioners are scientifically trained, however, in another direction. They have seen the play of unseen currents of energy upon and through the physical organism, and, having seen the results following certain mental procedures, they have gathered all the knowledge possible concerning those techniques, and since they are thorough students, they are thus laying the foundation for what will eventually become an accepted science of the mind.

Another thing—they do not base their work upon the older method of deductions from symptomatology. The doctor has to follow signs and symptoms, observed through the media of eye, ear, fingers, and laboratory equipment, then piece together the picture to give him a complete story of the physical condition. In the Science of Mind, we also train our practitioners to observe closely from the outer as a guide to the inner, but many practitioners of other schools say, "I do not wish to hear any description of symptoms." They will then give the treatment, completely ignoring physical signs and symptoms, ignoring equally that which the doctor has told the client about his condition.

This type of practitioner gets away from one difficulty. If the doctor's prognosis has been that the condition is incurable, the practitioner does not have the added burden of combatting something which has been accepted as hopeless by a doctor. Instead, he draws the client mentally to him, envelops him in the highest spiritual consciousness of which he is capable, and begins to treat for the very highest manifestation of the Godhead in this person; therefore, in his approach there would be no need of listening to the recital of symptoms.

THE UNIVERSAL HEALING PRINCIPLE

THESE THINGS ARE mentioned to show that there are different approaches to this method of healing, but they all come together at one point. Whether he listens to symptoms or not; whether he thinks of different conditions as difficult or easy to treat; whether he allows his clients to consult a doctor or take medicine or not, all practitioners draw their work down to one definite point, which is that there is a Universal Healing Principle at work, operating in some way within all men; that this invisible, perfect, inward Healing Presence operates in and through the physical structure of this person; moreover, that it acts as the result of definite mental work done on behalf of the client by the practitioner.

So we know that there is a method of healing through thought which can be used successfully by those who know the laws of thought, even though they might not be trained in the structure and function of the organs of the body.

MIND AND BODY

BASIC TO THIS belief is the fact that there is a flow of energy in and through the organism of a kind that is so adapted to the protoplasm that it can influence and mold it. Conversely, the tissues are evidently so constructed that they can be played upon and affected by this particular form of energy. There is apparently some affinity between thought and flesh, as between rubber cement and rubber, which allows for amalgamation between the two. In fact, thought and flesh are basically the same, except that they are in different form. If they were different, the one could not affect the other.

It might be better understood by thinking of a Servel and a Frigidaire. Both are refrigerators, but one is operated by a gas flame and the other by electricity. Neither will work by the flow of energy that operates the other. The flow of power through the mechanism must be so adapted to the mechanism, and the mechanism must be of a nature to respond to that sort of power. Otherwise there is no result.

So the fact that physical healing is possible by the flow of thought speaks of a connection between the nature of the two which makes the healing a scientific procedure.

Now here we have a human body. Man has discovered that there are currents of energy flowing through it. Moreover, he has found that without any material intervention whatever, merely as a result of the directing and the alteration of that flow of this particular kind of energy there is a bodily alteration corresponding in some way to the flow and to its direction. As a result, man has found that this energy is in some way concerned with his own thought. One thing that we know is that when the healing manifests, it comes in the last analysis in the way that the individual thinks of life. His own thought is the final stage in that healing.

"Well," someone says, "if that is the case, one has only to change his thought." This is partly true. But we add another thing at this point. We say that as man changes his thought, he must have some Absolute to which he will change it. There must be some perfect pattern.The most perfect picture man could hold, the most complete concept he could entertain of what he would call perfection, must be woefully inadequate and incomplete; so if there is to be healing, there must be somewhere a perfect pattern. This we believe to be held in the Mind of the Infinite. We believe further that it is the flow of thought-energy, originating in and coming from the Infinite Mind, which eventually heals the condition.

MEANING OF THE CHRIST

THE NAME THAT has been given to this Absolute is *The Christ.* It is a great pity that the term "Christ" has become so badly misunderstood. Modern Christians have the term tied in with religious associations, and when they hear the word, they immediately have one of two reactions. Either they assume a churchy or a reverent attitude, or they turn away scornfully, saying, "Don't hand me any of that stuff. I want none of it."

It would be much easier to explain the Christ to savages who had never heard of Christianity, for then one could explain to them what this healing Christ is that is in all men. Their reaction would be entirely different from ours. We are not always aware of the vast subjective field of association that is opened and becomes active within us at the mention of the word and that colors our emotional response to it.

The fact is that long before Jesus of Nazareth was born, the Christ was the name for the Divine Wisdom. It was not applied to any particular individual. But twenty centuries of its use as part of the name of the founder of Christianity has misled us as to its real and proper meaning and significance. It was not originally part of his name. He was born and named Jesus *Bar*-Joseph, meaning Jesus, son of Joseph. He was not named Jesus Christ. The people of his day knew him as Jesus of Nazareth. Later, the organized church called him Jesus the Christ, later shortened to Jesus Christ, because he gave evidence of being filled with the Absolute Wisdom to a higher degree than any individual who had ever lived, and of being a clear, open channel for the flow of Divine Wisdom, Intelligence, Love, Peace, and Power.

Consequently, men have gained the false impression that the name Christ signifies something which is peculiar to Jesus. It is not. The Christ Wisdom was known for ages before his time.

It is to be hoped that we shall not be misunderstood if we say that men would better understand the Christ by substituting the word "nature." While not entirely accurate, it would be much nearer the truth. The physician is really referring to the Christ when he uses the word "nature." He says that while he treats the patient, it is "nature" or "God" that heals. He is fully cognizant of the fact that there is at this moment within every cell, within every organ, and within the body as a whole an Infinite Wisdom which is doing easily and effortlessly what we with all our intelligence could not do. He says that this is what heals. He usually calls it nature.

PHYSICAL CONDITIONS HEALED

TWO RECENT INSTANCES illustrate this. Persons who had been treated by a spiritual practitioner surprised their physicians by showing no trace of the condition for which they had been going to them. The doctors expressed their surprise at the recoveries and said something like this: "Well, that shows how nature sometimes takes hold of these things and clears them up unaided." The fact is that the "Christ" of the spiritual practitioner and "nature" of the physician are one and the same thing. If we can get away from the churchy feeling at the mention of the Christ, we shall better understand this divine Principle through which healing is accomplished.

LIMITLESSNESS OF THE CHRIST

THERE IS A religious idea involved, but not a churchy superstition. The Christ is ageless and eternal. It operated eons before Jesus and will operate eons after we are gone. It was not something given once to one man only, for it is in all men forever.

The Christ is not limited to any one system of belief, nor is it bound to one creed, race, or color. It operates equally in men of all sorts and conditions, and in all religions, even those which deny it. The proof of this is seen in the fact that a cut finger in any of them is healed in precisely the same manner by the Christ Wisdom, or Nature, which in its Infinite Knowledge understands the mechanics of laying down cell after cell to heal the wound; therefore, the Christ of healing is not confined to any particular creed, cult, or sect. Some "believers" might be shocked to learn that it operates in the atheist, but when they come to realize that Christ is not a religious person, but the wisdom of nature, they will be able to reconcile their observational belief with their religious faith.

In point of time, the Christ is eternal. Stretch out time far into the past or the future; there never was a day when the Christ was not healing, and there never will be a day when it ceases to heal. Stretch out space way beyond the farthest star, the same Christ is there; and if there were need for healing, it would be operating as the healing agency exactly as it does here. In point of power, the Christ is limitless. Nothing that is ever presented to it is bigger than it is. Regardless of the trepidation with which we mortals might approach a situation, there is never a condition anywhere that is beyond the circle of its power or from which it would shrink, for its power is effortless, since it knows its own limitless resources.

THE BODY MAINTAINED IN HEALTH

BUT WHILE IT IS doing the more spectacular work of healing that which man calls disease, it is momentarily performing the even greater miracle of health. These fragile, delicate, easily upset bodies are maintained in balance by the healing Christ, so that in the majority of persons there is a reasonable degree of well-being. At this moment, Wisdom is performing in billions of earth-dwellers the incredible mysteries of digestion and metabolism, whereby it takes the food and, by an elusive system which in certain stages is incomprehensible, breaks it up into minute parts and builds its elements into actual flesh and blood, so that the food becomes the personal body. A mystery and a miracle if ever there was one.

Take the miracle of breathing. No one knows exactly how it is carried on. The doctor can explain what is happening, how the motor impulses carried over the nerves cause the diaphragm to rise and fall, forcing air into and out of the lungs. But no one knows exactly how the nerve impulses originate and why it is that they are started sixteen times every minute. Every breath that man draws is a miracle, but we accept it as a commonplace. It can even be called a miracle of healing, since healing is to keep whole, and this operation keeps the organism whole.

It might be of comfort to someone to know that this is all done so easily and effortlessly as to indicate a power that knows no impossible; therefore, if one is depressed because he has been told his condition is incurable, he might remember that in him *now* is a Wisdom, deep within his body, having a knowledge so comprehensive as to the rebuilding process that it knows how to rebuild completely any cell and bring it back to proper function. The healing of any condition, therefore, is entirely possible as far as the eternal Wisdom is concerned. It remains for us to bring our belief up to the level upon which the Infinite already acts.

WHERE THE REAL HEALING LIES

THERE IS MORE to be said about the Christ, because healing is more than the correction of a physical abnormality. This is where many have missed the path. Naturally, the condition which bothers us physically shrieks for attention; it is close to us; we want to get rid of it. On the other hand, our moral and ethical deformity or insufficiency causes us less concern, because the world does not see it, or it does not cause us too great discomfort. Because of this, man has stressed physical healing to a lopsided degree. He has said, "If my changed thought can change my body, I am going to change it." He has failed to see that true healing is the making whole of the entire man. A person who is healed is made whole.

A dishonest man is not whole, nor is he whole who is greedy, critical, gossipy, jealous, stingy, sensitive, easily hurt, prejudiced, or intolerant; therefore, in seeking only the physical healing because it hurts us, while persisting in our negative attitudes which bother others, we are double-minded. "The double-minded man is unstable in all his ways." The bifocused mind does not produce wholeness. "If one's eye be single, his whole body shall be full of light"—it shall be healed. Healing follows the unification of the whole man, and a single-focused mind is a healed mind.

The individual would be a far happier person if he were whole at all points. He would be more joyous if he were following the law of love, if he were cultivating those attitudes in which he was deliberately and "with benevolence aforethought" encircling others and thinking kindly of them. When the tendency is to tear others to shreds in our thoughts, if not verbally, over weaknesses in them which irk us, we should painstakingly search for the one good thing in them, deliberately withholding our criticism, loving those who in themselves are unlovable. The one who does this is filling in another segment of his personal circle, the final result of which is wholeness for himself, or healing.

We have not time to go into all the mental, moral, and ethical points at which this might be done, but it can be summed up by saying that the person who is healed through the Science of Mind method becomes a whole person, and if his healing is genuine instead of partial, he will become kinder and more accommodating; he will become more generous in his attitudes and will make more allowances for the less pleasant person stumbling blindly along the pathway of life. He will be a more mellow person than the ordinary man. In fact, such an alteration in his attitudes would tend to improve his physical condition, even though he knew nothing of the Science of Mind.

THE CHRIST IS THE KNOWER

THE CHRIST WISDOM in man is also the Knower. Man gets the furrows in his brow because he thinks of himself as confronted with problems too big for him to understand and handle. He fears to make a decision because of the possibility of loss. The Christ that is fully conversant with the way to make an enzyme for digesting starches is as fully informed upon what man calls his business or domestic problem. Again we are dealing with an Intelligence that knows no limit. There is nothing unseen or unknown to it. The same Wisdom that knows how to build the delicate linings of the tiny bronchials knows the answer to the situation confronting him elsewhere. It is the same Wisdom that flows through the mind of every successful businessman or housewife.

Thus man begins to add knowledge to his faith. It is good to have a simple faith, but it is better to have an intelligent faith. The world is richer for those simple souls who have said, "Just trust God and everything will come out all right," but after repeated setbacks and bafflement they have become puzzled and have wondered if God has not let them down. Some of them have eventually thrown up all belief in a good God. They failed to see that the more intelligent understanding they get of this that works within them, the better able they are to face the mysteries of life.

This Infinite Wisdom projected in man becomes the mind of man. There are undreamed-of depths to man's mind. The answer to every problem lies hidden there somewhere in its deeper levels. But man becomes panicky; the winds of his surface emotions whip up his conscious mind until his true knowledge has no chance to assert itself. Then, having made a mistake, he has less confidence in his judgment next time, and the vicious cycle repeats itself. During all this time the Knower rests quietly within him and at any point would have guided his judgment so long as he did not give way to fear, for the thing that is twisted and tangled to our panicky human view is a straight line to the Infinite Knower "stretched in smiling repose."

BE STILL; STAND STILL

TWO VERSES IN the Old Testament give us a key to the method which can be employed to allow the Knower to know through us. The first is "*Be still* and *know* that I am God." The second is "*Stand* still, and *see* the salvation of the Lord."

Who is God? The Christ *in* man; Nature; Wisdom; Intelligence; Love, Peace. All these are ways in which the Father is manifested in man, for God is the Absolute of which man's partial experience of these qualities is the relative. One can be still as he realizes that God is within him manifesting as these values.

But crisis arises, and we have to do something. If mentally we have not cultivated the ability to *be* still, we shall find it hard to *stand* still and see this thing clarify itself. Instead we begin to run around mentally, becoming more and more distraught.

But when we learn to cultivate an attitude that within us is a Knower that carries the answer to this thing, and that therefore there is no problem, we can then stand still and see the salvation of the Lord. Standing still does not mean inaction. We are using the best judgment of which we are capable, using the soundest business principles we know, but standing still mentally with an unexcited assurance that the Knower within has it all straight, and that we are being led through an unafraid use of our best judgment to the correct decision. Thus the Knower has a chance to act through the unhurried judgment of what we call "our" mind.

It must be a confident attitude, devoid of fear. Fear always twists the judgment. We should never make a decision when under the influence of fear. It's a wrong one from the start, for it is not the knowledge of the unafraid Knower. *Be still and know. Stand still and see.*

THE CHRIST IS THE HARMONIZER

THE CHRIST IS also the Harmonizer, constantly bringing together those persons, places, and things that are in harmony and gently or violently separating those things that cease to be in harmony. This is why the person who entertains bitterness and rancor will find that he draws inharmony into his affairs. The healing of the condition comes from opening up to the Harmonizing Christ. We do not have to change others, but ourselves; the others will change and become cooperative when we do.

THE CHRIST IS THE OPENER

THE CHRIST IS also the Opener of gates. Man runs into brick walls during his passage through life. He would like to gain entry here, or open up a source of business or income there, but the way is barred. The harder he batters at the walls, the less inclined they seem to open. The Infinite Christ is the Opener. At whatever point one finds himself shut away from his good, he has within him that which will open the gateway to it. It does not call for "storming the gates," for it is "not by might, nor by power, but by my Spirit, saith the Lord." But it all comes back again to "*Be* still" and "*Stand* still." Inward restfulness coupled with sensible industry is the key.

THE PERSONAL AND THE IMPERSONAL

PEOPLE ARE SOMETIMES shocked by our use of the pronoun "It" applied to the Christ. They will use it freely in regard to Nature or Intelligence but shrink from using it with reference to the Christ. The inflexibility of this great Law of Nature demands that we recognize its impersonalities; therefore we say "It." The Christ is always subjective, impersonal, operating under the impulses of that which we call "Our Father." God—warm, personal, part of us, and we part of Him—and the Christ, the Absolute standard that is set, operating by law, impersonal, filled with all intelligence and with all creative power, always operating to follow out the word of the Father. When God said, "Let there be light," it was the Christ that made it possible for Him to say, "And there was light." It is our understanding of this relationship which enables us to live intelligently.

ESTABLISHING THE RELATIONSHIP

THIS RELATIONSHIP IS established through scientific prayer. Even when others have prayed in ways in which we have not prayed, where the prayer has followed these principles, they have had their answer. Such externals as facing the east, kneeling, clasping the hands, or ending with the words "In Jesus' name" are all inconsequential. The fundamentals which make prayer an actual force that brings answers are hidden in the words "Be still and know that within you is a Healing Christ that has never been baffled, that is able to solve this situation." Then, don't be jittery; stand still quietly within yourself, knowing that the Infinite Healing Presence never has to be begged or placated; it has only to be recognized.

Man has been as one in a deep sleep, dreaming nightmares and experiencing the nightmares of his sleep. As he comes to the place of the open eye, he sees that right here within him now the Healing Presence is altering conditions as he allows it to operate in his stillness. Thus the secret of healing is hidden from no one.

How to Get Along with Troublesome People

Ah God! that men would see a little clearer,
Or judge less harshly where they cannot see!
Ah God! that men would draw a little nearer
To one another—they'd be nearer Thee,
And understood.
—THOMAS BRACKEN, "Not Understood"

MOST PHILOSOPHIES INTENDED to produce inner tranquillity have one drawback—they call for withdrawal from the world of men. The cloistered life, sheltered from the impact of other personalities, might have seemed desirable in past centuries, but today man needs a philosophy which will enable him to live in the hurly-burly of the modern world, surrounded by people rather than withdrawn from them, advancing upon life's problems rather than retreating from them.

We are tied up in the bundle of life with others. Each has ends he wishes to gain, a personality that differs from our own, curious and diverse standards of ethics and morals, and perhaps mannerisms that irk us. But they are here, and we must learn how to get along with them, in the home, office, factory, and across national boundaries.

If we can find a logical, fair, and sensible approach to those who cross our path and whose divergent aims seem to be at cross-purposes with our own, we might find the way to international as well as personal "peace with dignity."

GETTING ALONG WITH ONESELF

THE FIRST THING that one has to learn in getting along with others is how to get along with his own difficult self. True, there are many disagreeable persons in the world; yet it must be admitted that much of our trouble with them comes from within us primarily, and from them only secondarily. Some hidden rage within us, of which we might be totally unaware, sets off in them the reactions from which we eventually suffer. Being hurt by their reaction, we accept the surface explanation and condemn them as being mean.

Looking deeper, the observant person can note that their animosity merely reflects his own frustration. For the most part, he who looks outside himself for the cause of his woes looks in the wrong direction; he who looks within for a hitherto hidden cause will often open the gates of an unsuspected prison and will open the way into the mastery of life.

The unadjusted person finds himself surrounded by unadjusted individuals. The uncooperative person attracts uncooperative attitudes from others. These are often tokens of his inner maladjustment rather than proofs of the ugliness of others. Well-adjusted people have little difficulty with others, for they attract harmony; inharmony finds it difficult to thrive in their atmosphere.

BADNESS IS BLINDNESS

People are sometimes puzzled when students of human nature declare that human nature is fundamentally good. They point to the almost universal selfishness, greed, and cruelty manifested on the personal, group, class, national, and international levels as evidence to the contrary. The reply is that while human nature basically is good, it is also blind.

Mankind generally is conscious of deep desires for security, love, happiness, comfort. The preponderant mass of men mistakenly believe that to achieve these goals they must push others away from them. In their blind fear that they will be left out, they act selfishly, sometimes cruelly. Passengers who have been gracious acquaintances during a voyage will strike and kick others out of the way during a shipwreck in order to get into the lifeboat. In the same way, the struggle for survival is responsible for the meanness of blinded persons in daily life. The supreme act of cruelty in the world's history was thus seen by its victim, who said, "Forgive them; they know not what they do." Wickedness is often a wrong aim rather than a wrong intention.

GUARDING AGAINST FRUSTRATION

MAN MUST GUARD against his inner frustrations, for through the law of cause and effect they are at the root of much of the unfair treatment he receives from others. Sooner or later, he is treated as he deserves rather than as he wishes. His inner turmoil sets off ugliness in others who, having less restraint, allow it to break forth into action.

The frustrated person is always unhappy deep within himself whether he reveals it to the world or not. He may show it by an attitude of complaint and criticism, or he may not; but the grass always looks greener on the other side of his fence.

He is envious; he says, "If only I had his money, looks, position, political influence, education, or family position—things come easy for him—he is lucky." The tendency is to think the other fellow is not faced with the problems that confront him, that the other's path is easy while his is hard.

He thinks he could do better with a different employer or fellow employees—that he could sell better in a different territory. If he has failed financially, he wants to overturn the economic system, hoping to get something better in the economic shuffle.

In one sense, he is an idealist, a perfectionist, but he is looking in the wrong direction for the cause of his failure to achieve his ideal. He looks everywhere but in the right place—within himself. Man best cleans up the world's wrongs by sweeping his own doorstep. Anything short of this is a flight from reality to fantasy.

Having moved mentally into the world of his ideal, dreaming of the accompanying enjoyment, he is brought up with a jerk by the realities of his insufficiency. His ability to dream plus his inability to achieve his end sets up a frustration which turns to hidden rage. He is blind, not bad. He wants a magic wand to dissolve his obstructions, grant all his wishes, make angels of those around him while leaving him to remain emotionally immature. It just cannot be done.

THE ATTITUDE OF THE WELL-ADJUSTED PERSON

On the other hand, the well-adjusted person does not demand absolute perfection in those about him, because he is clearly aware of his own imperfection.

The maladjusted says, "I am unhappy because others are not kind and cooperative with me. Nobody helps me. I might as well end it all," or "Let's have a revolution and overthrow the whole system."

The adjusted person says, "I have the same difficulties because I live in a world of imperfect humans. I see much to criticize, but I go ahead, trying to do my daily stint." He does what he can, endeavoring to adjust himself to ugliness where it shows up, knowing that neither he nor his neighbors are all that they should be.

All persons are a little abnormal at some point. This is a bitter pill, but the well-adjusted person swallows it. Our own peculiarities have been so long with us that they seem normal. Our own views seem to be unbiased; yet we all are unconsciously slanted in specific directions. Our early conditioning colors our interpretation of the experience no matter how objective we try to be.

When the maladjusted person finds turmoil appearing in

his affairs, he asks, "Why do people do these things to *me*?" The adjusted person asks, "*What* in me might be stirring this up in them? Have I been thinking in terms of cross-purposes, obstructions and animosities at *some other point* in my affairs? Are these seeping through into my outer life to show themselves in the disagreeable actions of others?"

Knowing that nothing can come into his life but that which he attracts either consciously or unconsciously, he begins to take note of little things which have crept in unnoticed—little irritations which normally would have been brushed aside or ignored, but which he has carelessly allowed to get under his skin. When he sweeps his own doorstep and checks these irritations, he finds things quieting down in those who surround him.

TREATMENT FOR INNER PEACE

IN THE SCIENCE of Mind, he would accomplish this by giving himself mental treatment, approximately as follows:

> *Peace must be the true state of man because Peace lies at the heart of the Infinite—quiet, deep, unruffled Peace.*
>
> *Since this is true, and my mentality is merely an extension of this Infinite Mind, then that which is true of the Infinite must be true of me.*
>
> *No person, place or thing has the power to irritate me without my consent. In my fathomless depths is the Infinite Peace. These ripples are only on the surface and are transient. This sense of hurt and irritation is not part of my true self; it does not belong to me and was never intended to be part of my experience. I send*

my love, tolerance, and kindliness in the direction of that irritation, and my new attitude dissolves everything unlike itself.

Practicing this tiny phase of the Law of Mental Action is usually sufficient to replace turmoil with peace, and this new attitude is reflected in others' cooperativeness where bitterness had been.

SENSITIVENESS AND SELF-PITY

Sensitiveness and self-pity are signs of emotional immaturity. The slave of self-pity is of all men most miserable, because he need never take more than a few steps beyond his front door to find someone giving him a look or a word which confirms his false belief that the world is against him.

This person is always on a "sensitivity defensive." This grows out of a sense of inadequacy although he does not know it. In one way, he has correctly analyzed himself and found himself wanting. Instead of building up his conviction of his own competency, he takes the easier attitude of expecting rejection from others. Instead of altering himself, he stands on the alert for criticism from others; his unconscious guilt sense makes him quick to read into the actions of others that which unconsciously exists only in the depths of his own subconscious mind. This puts him in an attitude of separation from them.

They, without reasoning it out, feel separated from him, therefore unresponsive to him; it is his own "atmosphere of separation" operating through them and attracting that which it is like. Thus his own sensitiveness brings that from which he shrinks. Moreover, even though others do nothing hostile, his "sensitivity defensive" makes him read hostility into innocent performance or good-natured teasing.

Assuming that we have arrived at the adjusted life, how shall we act toward troublesome persons? Even the emotionally mature run into those who are uncooperative, quarrelsome, selfish, tearful, or explosive when trying to get their own way. Should we yield to them, or resist? There is a proper way to handle these persons.

PITY DISSOLVES ANGER

TWO ATTITUDES ARE helpful—pity and decisiveness, equally balanced. Walking through the mountain pine growths, one is struck by the fact that most pines grow straight and true, but one here and there is crooked and deformed. To the natural inquiry, the forester answers that some outside influence exerted itself while that tree was a sapling—a heavy stone, perhaps a fence post that is no longer there. The cause has gone; the effect remains.

This person was not born with an evil disposition. All children are naturally loving; they crave and give affection freely. Some influence must have played upon this one to turn him sour. Had we been subjected to it, we too should have grown up with this kind of disposition. So our first emotion is pity—pity that what was intended to be a thing of beauty has become deformed through the play of life upon it, and thankfulness that we were spared those warping childhood influences, or that we have been able to correct our attitudes and live normally with others.

Our pity would keep us from criticism, hatred, or trying to get even with the warped mentality. One would not hate a person who had an ugly physical deformity; he would be thankful he had been spared it.

MEANNESS IS UNHAPPINESS

This distorted personality must be abjectly unhappy within himself, for he is twisted away from the normal attitudes to his fellows. He is out of line with the stream of life, filled with a seething unrest, not knowing how to attain peace. Often he attacks those who have been kindest to him, for their inner peace and evident adequacy throw his unrest into bold relief. If he cannot come up to their quiet, he tries to bring them down to his turmoil. He does not do this consciously; he would violently deny it, but his actions show that it is an unconscious desire, for they result in turmoil to those about him. Misery loves company!

The adjusted person does not give tit for tat when hurt, because that would be to drop down to the level upon which this unhappy one lives; thus he would be tuned in to the same mental frequency and would become enmeshed in the negative mental states of the other. As long as he remains aloof, he circles upon a higher plane, detached from negative contact, and can thus help the other. The man who stands well braced on the pier can pull the drowning man out, whereas they might both drown if he jumped into the water with the rope.

Man possesses a faculty by which he need never be hurt by anything done by anyone else. He can rise above any shafts aimed at him, taking a selfless position where he refuses to accept anything of a hurtful nature as personal. Whenever he allows himself to be hurt, he has descended from this impregnable position, and his angry tone indicates that he has allowed himself to drop to the level of the neurotic. The integrated individual refuses to do this. His inner calm is his unassailable citadel. No one else can storm it. Only he can surrender it. This he refuses to do, even under great provocation. He has pity for those who surrender.

STAND QUIETLY FIRM

BUT HE IS DECISIVE also. Knowing that this person has been conditioned to believe that he can get his wishes by storming, tears, or tantrums, and knowing that he must not be encouraged in this false belief, the adjusted person faces him with firmness, refusing to yield in order to prevent a scene. Every tantrum that succeeds in producing what the person wants merely confirms him in the notion that his way is right and makes him more troublesome.

But not all neurotics rave and scream. There is the "sweet," soft-spoken person who gets her way by silent weeping, fainting spells, or "heart attacks" when she can't have her way. Her subtle approach makes others feel brutally unkind and is quite effective. The feminine gender is used here, because it is found more often in women, as the explosive technique is found more often in men.

THE CURSE OF SELF-LOVE

THE CHIEF CHARACTERISTIC of troublesome persons is that they want their own way. Others exist only to cater to their wishes. Whether noisy or silent, they are dictators at heart. Self-love is stronger than love of others. They do for others only those things which feed their own ego; they frequently use the phrase "After all I have done for you." They believe in lofty self-sacrifice for others but do not practice it themselves. When persuading someone to do something for them, they promise eternal gratitude, which lasts only until they want the next favor, when the whole cycle starts all over again. They make the giver feel heartless unless he gives in; so he surrenders to avoid a scene.

There is no appeasement of their appetite, because it feeds upon its own gratification. Finally, after one has yielded repeatedly and now takes his stand, saying "No more," the scene comes anyway, proving that appeasement never gains gratitude.

The normal person is always ready to help a friend in distress; this is as it should be. The above comments refer only to the habitual parasite. Unselfish assistance helps the average person along the road he is manfully trying to negotiate under his own power. One of life's primary lessons is that each must learn to stand on his own feet, facing his problems as far as possible alone. He who receives help too easily and too frequently soon learns that this method is easier than self-propulsion. Constant assistance fosters this false view and is destructive to his best character development.

EVADING RESPONSIBILITY

IT HAS ALWAYS BEEN true that man is on a voyage of exploration. He is a vast continent of undiscovered resources, gifts, powers. Some hover timidly or lazily along the shores, content to have the more robust souls penetrate the uncertain hinterland and bring back the good things of life. They must be taught that they have responsibilities, for they are part of the bundle of humanity on the ocean of life. Both they and their neighbors have oars, and they have to pull their share. It is not enough to say, "I am tired and I have a blister"; the others are tired and have blisters too. Everybody has blisters. Everybody gets tired; but life rewards courage and persistence with more courage; thus character develops.

The integrated person has thoughtfully developed an intelligent approach to the various sides of life from which trouble is likely to arise. He has worked out the proper attitudes toward his health, money, work, ethics, morals, and friendships, so that his attitudes can be fair to himself and at the same time fair and human toward his neighbor. This becomes his life policy. Business houses succeed where they have a definite business policy; so does the individual.

Once his policy is decided upon, it becomes his plan for successful living. He is wise never to depart from it under the pressure of others, nor will he seek to impose his ideas upon others. He takes his stand upon the following: "I will never impose upon anyone beyond that which I would expect him to impose upon me," and conversely, "I will not allow anyone to impose upon me beyond that which I would impose upon him." This makes for decision of character; anything else makes for wobbly-mindedness. Clear thinking produces clear acting; muddy thinking makes for muddy acting.

A REASONABLE PHILOSOPHY OF LIFE

THIS IS A REASONABLE philosophy of life. It means that we recognize the inviolability of the human personality. No one has the right to invade the individuality of another and expect him to break up his pattern of life to cater to the insufficiencies of the former. This may sound like harsh doctrine to the escapist and the clinger; on the contrary it is eminently fair, because the person practices it coming and going. He will not impose upon, but he demands the same immunity for himself. He does not say that they shall live by his pattern, but he insists that they shall not make him live by theirs.

"But," someone asks, "is not one boorish in refusing to go along with the neurotic?" Not if he retains a cheerful, noncensorious attitude toward the other. He refuses to hate or criticize him, but he also refuses to cater to his neurosis.

"No" can be uttered with either a falling or a rising inflection. The former is sometimes called the "banker's no," althought this is a slander upon most bankers. The latter is the "No" with which one says he takes no sugar in his coffee—quite decisive, but with no criticism of those who take sugar. There is no personal pleasure in refusing, no gloating, no feeling that one has handed him just what he deserves. We are completely friendly to him, but not to his false attitude toward life.

Shakespeare spoke deep truth when he made Polonius say:

To thine own self be true,
And it must follow, as the night the day,
Thou canst not then be false to any man.

The most valuable man is he who, having set an ideal, remains true to it in spite of another's anger and vituperation. His steadiness helps those who grope blindly toward self-sufficiency, in the long run, even though at the moment they may accuse him of being selfish, heartless, and of "breaking my heart."

But there must be no inward apology for his attitudes. He

must really be sold on his pattern of life. Otherwise he will only alienate and do no good, for his inward uncertainty will register in the mind of the other.

Getting along with troublesome people is simply being as true as one can to his inner ideals. The world is full of people who would switch him onto side tracks, offering the most specious arguments to support their view. If he is sure that his ideals have been conceived in a spirit of fairness to all, if he can stand by them without inner apology on the one hand or acrimony on the other, then that which is best for him eventually turns out to be best for all those whose lives are affected by his decisions.

What Is This Power That Heals?

MENTAL AND SPIRITUAL healing is by no means a modern fad. It is as old as the human race. Sacred and secular history cites thousands of instances in ancient and modern times in which the healing of the physical body has been accomplished without any material intervention whatever. Intermittently appearing in human experience, it runs like a scarlet thread throughout man's history. There is ample proof that there is a Healing Principle in the universe which can deal with the most serious maladies when properly contacted.

The hard-bitten materialist has brushed aside these healings as products of overwrought imaginations; consequently there has not been, until comparatively recently, any serious effort to conduct extensive research into the nature of the Power that heals. Engrossed in the study of the atom, scientific man has neglected the study of the marvelous mind that has been able to build machines with which to study his universe and has seemed loath to explore the Greater Mind which locked that terrific power within the atom; therefore, it has been left to men of a more spiritual approach. In one way this has been providential, for study of this Power reveals that it is a Spiritual Power to be spiritually approached.

APPROACHES TO HEALING

TWO APPROACHES HAVE been made to healing through the mind.

One was popularized by Sigmund Freud toward the end of the nineteenth and the early part of the twentieth century. One could not possibly explain the Freudian theory in the short space at our disposal. It is sufficient to say that the treatment seeks to resolve the unconscious conflicts that lie beneath the surface of man's apparent desires. It is a distinctly psychological approach, although modern psychologists in the main are by no means Freud-worshippers.

Freud's research, however, laid the foundation for a system of psychotherapy now being quite generally accepted by the medical profession and called psychosomatic (mind and body) medicine. This moves at a tangent from Freud but nevertheless approaches the problem from his distinctly humanistic point of view without any particular spiritual or religious coloring. Excellent healings have been reported from this method.

The other approach is that with which we deal. It regards

man as being the mentality within the body, the living person, an eternal entity who, as mind, is made in the image and likeness of God, which means that he, as mind, is in the small that which Supreme Mind must be in the large. It believes that a twofold seeking is always going on: man seeking union with his Source, and the Source always seeking expression through man. It believes that the Universal Healing Principle is some phase of the Infinite Mind and that when man is successful in establishing rapport with the Infinite Mind, it becomes for him an Infinite Healing Presence.

Our approach takes cognizance of anything discovered by psychology regarding the way in which the human mind tangles itself; yet it is not a psychological method. It endeavors to establish a distinctly spiritual contact, but not necessarily a churchy or theological one.

EVIDENCE OF THE POWER AT WORK

THE PRIMARY PURPOSE of religion has always been to establish spiritual contacts, although it must be confessed that the church in large areas and sometimes for centuries has lost sight of this purpose; therefore, it follows that most of the spiritual healings have come through some sort of uncomplicated religious practice.

The Roman Catholic shrines of Canada, France, and other parts of the world have on record many well-authenticated instances of healing through this spiritual approach. The members of the Medical Bureau at Lourdes lean over backward in their unwillingness to certify a case as healed without the most stringent examination before and after the reported healing. Any physician of any faith, even a professed atheist, can study and examine the patients. In fact, many patients whom they would discharge as cured in their home practice are rejected by this bureau as not cured. Yet many true healings have been certified.

It is quite understandable that any man would be skeptical, trained as he is in the scientific method, knowing the hardness of tissue compared to the seeming insubstantiality of man's thought. It is not unreasonable that a man should doubt that a leg would grow to the point where the steel extension shoe would not be needed, or that a ruptured abdominal wall should be re-knit through the agency of thought. Yet in shrines around the world I have seen the shoes hung on the walls, along with the trusses, crutches, and other medical appurtenances which had been discarded following the healing of the condition.

Man has been conditioned to accept some things as belonging completely to the physical realm; therefore, it is difficult to believe that actual changes in physical tissue can be brought about by what the race in general has too often considered to be some mysterious hocus-pocus.

DR. CARREL ON THE POWER

BUT IS IT hocus-pocus? One famous man, internationally recognized as an authority on biological processes, spent time at the shrine at Lourdes, impartially observing those who came for healing. Dr. Alexis Carrel could not be called gullible; his whole life would refute that charge; yet he was not blindly wedded to the materialistic notion that physical tissue could not be changed by an intangible force.

He stated his considered opinion to be that there is a

definite healing force flowing throughout the universe and within ordinary men and women. He said further that this force, not being measurable by any of the accepted yardsticks of science, must be apprehended by some other method. He added one observation, which was that this healing force flows as a result of the cultivation of specific attitudes, one of which is prayer. He saw a cancerous growth disappear, which he watched, and stated that there is no known biological or physiochemical law by which this could have taken place; therefore, he assumed that there must be some spiritual law that transcends any of the known laws of the universe and whose action is invoked by the spiritual activity called "prayer."

Dr. Carrel knew there is a Power that heals. He probably had a good idea as to what this Power is, but, lacking scientific terms in which to state it, he was forced to fall back upon that word which embraces Supreme Intelligence, Wisdom, Power, and Creativeness—namely, God. A healing such as he had observed does not take place wholly in the imagination. Some positive and definite action is needed to replace destructive cells with living, healthy cells. Things don't just happen. Something or someone makes them happen; for every effect there has to be an adequate and sufficient cause.

MORE EVIDENCE OF THE POWER AT WORK

IN A HEART DISORDER

A man suddenly collapsed in his office from a heart disorder. The next thing he knew he was in the hospital under oxygen, while the doctor was telling his wife that he had grave doubts that they could pull him through. A spiritual practitioner who was not limited by the belief in "incurability" was contacted, and the man was back at his desk within a few weeks instead of the six months or more that is usually considered imperative in such a case if the patient survives. Almost five years have gone by without a recurrence. Neither the attack nor the recovery was imaginary. Some definite Power was brought into play.

IN LOVE AND MARRIAGE

A woman came to a spiritual practitioner and said, "I am lonely and wish I had a mate. But I know I am not glamorous. All my life I have been passed by for women who I know are not as capable homemakers, nor who have as good dispositions as I." She told the truth, for she was quite plain and unattractive, nearing middle age. Yet there was a certain type of man for whom she would be the ideal wife, a man who valued inner beauty highest and who wanted the quiet steadiness which was evidently her most valuable asset.

Not long after that, she drew into her life a man who was one of the salt of the earth. He was a quiet, unassuming, well-doing man of good habits, a few years widowed, not wealthy but in comfortable circumstances. A few years have passed, and their home has been a place of enrichment for both.

IN ALCOHOLISM

A man of fifty had been a steady, persistent drinker for twenty-five years but had been a periodical for the last eight or ten of those years. He had brains, ability, and charming personality, but he had been let out of good companies because he went on sprees lasting about three weeks. His ability as a manufacturing executive caused his employers to overlook the first one or two slips, but eventually they were forced to discharge him.

Today this man holds a responsible position with a large corporation and has had no desire for liquor for over seven years.

IN FINANCES

We have seen salesmen rapidly change from bringers of alibis into bringers of orders, businesses that were headed for the rocks revitalized, men and women working for small wages coming to own their own prosperous businesses. These persons have been able definitely to alter distinctly material conditions to a degree that indicates that there is a definite Power which enters into the picture and produces the change.

CONTACTING THE POWER

HEALING HAS TO DO primarily with the belief of the person, in which a false belief is healed with a consequent right-about-face in the way he regards the universe. He now views his material world as subservient to his mental and spiritual world, knowing that his thought patterns determine the shape and conditions of his little universe as the thought of the Supreme Intelligence determines the shape and pattern of the universe at large. This shift is significant in that it places the field of causes within himself, where he can control them, instead of in the outer world, where he cannot do much about them.

Since the healing of a false belief is the basic healing, it does not seem to matter in what field this belief operates. The inward attitude is primary; the particular manifestation is secondary. Thus one finds the term "healing" applied also to business and personal problems.

FOR ALCOHOLISM

Earlier we mentioned a man who had been a heavy drinker. How was this Power introduced to heal him of this habit?

He was shown that the excessive drinker is always running away from life at some point. He is not yet completely assured of his own manhood, his ability to stand alone at every single point in his experience.

In his case, it developed that he shrank from the adverse opinions of other men. He said, "I've always wanted to be known as a man among men." He had thought that if he refused to drink with others, they would regard him as a sissy, which he assuredly was not; he was a real man's man. But this fear was his real disease; his drinking was only its manifestation.

He did not need treatment to take away the physical appetite for liquor. This had been done for him several times in institutions.

What he needed was something deeper; he needed an inner sense of his own worth regardless of what others thought of him.

He was asked, "What happens when you drink?" to which he replied, "After I have had a few I feel 'high.' I have plenty of courage. I feel that I am as good as anyone who lives. I am ready to tackle anything.''

He was then shown that if liquor could bring his thinking up to that level, his mind had the ability to think in that quality, and that the stimulus could be his own logical reasoning instead of a drug. What he needed was a consciousness of his own adequacy and sufficiency *as a man*.

Other people's opinion would not make him a man even though they slapped him on the back and told him so. Their opinion would not make him any less a man when he refused a drink as long as within himself he knew that he had come to know his true worth.

He was guided to bring his mind toward all the places at which he had shown or could show his real ability when placed in competition with others. This took him several days. Finally, he had made out a quite respectable list of his good qualities, places where he had proved himself, commendations from colleagues or superiors, his honesty, his willingness to stick to a difficult thing until he had put it through, his pride in his wife who had stuck with him through thick and thin, his money-making qualities, and a number of other points peculiar to his own life and affairs.

Then he was shown that the physical tissues do not come to crave alcohol, as many mistakenly think, regardless of how long or how steadily one has been a drinker. The physical tremors and ''jitters'' that the reformed drinker has are not evidence of physical craving; they are evidence of the frayed nerves which the drinking has caused and which steady alcoholizing merely narcoticized into passivity. They quickly regain their vitality and become a better telegraph system over which the brain can send its messages in the future.

He had to be shown that it is mental craving. The hand

itself cannot reach out until the mind tells it to do so. Man builds pictures within his mentality of the desirability of drinking, then transmits these pictures along the nerves to the feet so that they make their way to a bar, then to the voice so that it calls for a drink, then to the hand so that it lifts the glass. It is mental from start to finish.

He came to see that there is an expulsive power in a new affection. He began to cultivate a love for the picture of himself as held in respect by others for his achievements, the joy of his wife, the happiness of their life together, the respect of his children, the financial future secure and progressing with the years, but best of all the warm inner feeling that he was *a man*, directing his desires rather than being directed by them.

He saw that he did not have to fight to overcome an appetite or a habit, but to cultivate an approach. When he did this, the habit dropped away, for there was no longer any necessity for it.

His thought was healed, for excessive drinking is a mental rather than a physical disease. Power flowed into his life when he began to see that the physical craving was only an effect; the real trouble lay deep within his mental attitudes. The change of them was the healing that allowed Infinite Power to complete the outward mastery.

The trouble is that men fight the habit itself, gritting their teeth and saying, "I hate you. I'm done with you. I'll never touch you again." This seems to call up some diabolical something within them that catches them on the rebound when the initial feeling wears off, and once more enslaves them. The method that builds upon one's true nature, that makes a man impervious to what anyone thinks of him, that makes him try to realize and live up to his true self—this is the true method, because it draws him in line with the underlying principle of that Power which heals. It now begins to operate within him and is the secret of his victory.

FOR LOVE AND MARRIAGE

We mentioned the woman who wanted marriage. How did she draw the Power into action in her behalf? By turning her thought away from what *she* wanted, toward the idea that somewhere there was some man for whom life had never been and could never be truly satisfactory until he faced it with her at his side.

She was shown that the first thing to be healed was her false belief. She had thought of her plainness whenever she thought of love, and her honesty told her that many men wanted more outer charm. This meant that whenever she thought of her desire she thought of herself as separated from it. She was told to think of love as something to which she was united rather than from which she was barred. It was suggested that she had been thinking of all the reasons why she could not draw love, instead of all the reasons why she could.

The word "repent" means to make a complete right-about-face, to disbelieve what has formerly been believed, to believe what has formerly been disbelieved. The healing is the repentance; the repentance is the healing.

She turned decisively away from what she did not have and began to think of what she did have to offer. She knew her own high intelligence, her wide interests, her deep sincerity, her sympathy, her sense of humor, her great capacity for affection, her good taste which would make a home attractive and comfortable. She knew that somewhere there was a man who had failed to find all these desirables in any woman he had met and whose nature was such that they all were important to him.

Then she turned to the idea that life is always trying to fulfill itself; it never leaves itself incomplete except as we build a concept of its incompleteness. She had used her lack of physical attractiveness to build a concept of unfulfillment.

But she went further! She convinced herself that her false belief was also shutting away from some man the good that he desired. This helped her to see herself as meeting another's need, rather than someone taking pity on her loneliness and consenting to marry her. This change alone brought in a new sense of her importance and of her desirability.

Most important of all, she began to think of herself as having an agent. Just as she would call in a realtor, tell him exactly what she wanted in a house and the amount of money she was able to exchange for it, then leave the finding of it to him, knowing that he knew where such a house was or how to go about finding one, she began to see the Infinite Mind as her Agent. She took the attitude that her desire for marriage was the movement of God within her, and that He, being omniscient, knew exactly where her type of man was. She laid the problem before the Infinite, but with this important difference: instead of thinking of all the reasons why someone might *not* marry her, as she had always done before when thinking of the subject, she was now stressing the reason why someone would greatly desire her.

Then she thought, "I know that somewhere there is the kind of man with whom I could be happy, and whom I do not have to change, for I like him as he is. Nor does he have to change me in any point, because he likes me exactly as I am. His good qualities correspond to the house I want; my good qualities correspond to the house I want; my good qualities are the price I am ready to pay. Since I've told the Agent about it I shall go about my daily duties, quietly knowing that I have put the transaction in the hands of the best Agent in the universe.''

Even God cannot bring good into the life of the person who persists in occupying himself with reasons why the good cannot come. The Law of Mind is a law of reflection. The mirror can flash back at us only that which we place in front of it. A quiet, intelligent faith in a spiritual law seems to draw the Power into the life, for even God cannot withhold the good when one has fulfilled the conditions. Nor would He want to.

FOR WORLD PROBLEMS

If an individual can restore harmony in the physical organism by restoring harmony within his own thought, then a nation can do it, and a world can do it.

The person healed through spiritual means always shows a new attitude toward others, a new gentleness and understanding. Hatred gradually or rapidly disappears from his thinking. The desire to crush or take advantage passes away. A new spirit of understanding enters. He enjoys the inner harmonies so well that he refrains from doing that which would disturb them in others, for that which he sets up in others he himself experiences.

Man is rapidly coming to understand the relative value of the inner and the outer and is beginning to see its relation to international problems. ''Wars and fightings'' come from the belief in the supremacy of the outer, the physical. The day will come when the world's thought will be healed and wars cease.

Peace can never come from superior armaments alone; true peace can come only from within the heart of mankind.

This awakening across the face of the world, at present only the first shafts of light preceding the sun's rising, will assuredly be followed by light that will drench mankind. Political Utopia is a cruel dream; spiritual Utopia is an imminent possibility. Wise men of spiritual understanding have forecast it throughout the ages. Today, in man's darkest hour, he is on the verge of realizing it. Man's false beliefs are reaching their logical end in the horrors of this rapidly changing world. The day of man's barbarism is dying with terrifying convulsions, that the day of his spiritual understanding may be born. A belief in the supremacy of the mental and spiritual is emerging, but it is the same message taught by Jesus and the Prophets that "It is done unto you as you believe."

This demands the quiet heart, the spirit of goodwill, the absence of hatred and cross-purposes. In the past, those who have practiced these virtues have been too often trampled underfoot by the conqueror or scorned as "impractical" by those who have lived by the rule of "Look out for number one." Today, as the hollowness of the materialistic philosophy makes itself evident, the practical good sense of the spiritual is emerging. In fact, the revival is now gathering momentum as the earth crisis approaches. Barbarism and spirituality are racing toward the fork in the road. Barbarism is now no longer far out in front; spirituality is catching up with giant strides and will overtake and turn it back. When it does, this earth will become as near a Paradise as anything touched with human imperfection can become. It will then be the vehicle through which this unseen Power freely operates.

World healing is part of the whole subject of healing, for nations have to be healed just as individuals do. War and hatred are the diseases of the body politic. The same Power that heals arthritis can heal war.

THE POWER ITSELF

AGAIN WE COME back to our thesis that there is an actual Power that enters in addition to man's changed thought. Man has wished for peace within his own body and among men since time began, but only recently has he come to see how it may be brought about. Now he is coming to understand that there is an actual Power which flows wherever the thinking is brought into line with the Power principle. Electricity has always existed, but it will never flow until the laws of its flow are met. The Infinite Power has always existed but usually has flowed only through those somewhat otherworldly men who have placed themselves in line with its method.

ITS TRANSCENDENCE

There is no limit to Infinite Power. Man is so accustomed to measuring power that he wonders whether there is enough power to heal desperate conditions. He must shake himself free of the self-limiting view which in turn limits the result. He must break away from the bonds of a belief in material obstructions and turn to a belief in an irresistible Power which moves silently, easily, and effortlessly in response to his thought. This Power must be to him something far and away beyond that of his human mentality or of the strongest will. It must be Originating Power, All-Power, God.

This is clearly illustrated by an incident that occurred more than three thousand years ago. We all remember the liberation of the Israelites from Egypt's bondage. They made their way across the sand to the shore of the Red Sea. Then, to their horror they saw the Egyptian chariots raising dust in the distance, coming to slaughter or to re-enslave. The Israelites could go neither forward nor backward. They were trapped. It is easy to imagine their panic, for at some time most persons have come to apparently hopeless situations like this in life.

As they milled around in their terror, the voice of their liberator rang out, clear and unafraid. Moses said, "Stand still, stand still, and see the salvation of the Lord." To the eyes of material sense this was the most foolish advice. Why did he not form them into battle lines as any sensible man would do? But he had a higher sense, for he had had enough experiences to know the tremendous Power that flows into the life once panic is removed. He probably moved among them, telling them to let their minds stand still, not alone their feet. When panic subsided, it is reported that the sea opened and allowed them to pass over in safety, and that as the Egyptians followed, the sea swept them into oblivion.

Scholars are divided as to whether this was an actual physical event in the life of the Hebrews. So often a biblical narrative uses only a slight basis in historical fact as a means of conveying some deeply spiritual truth.

If this is one such, it certainly carries inspiration for the person confronted with a deep crisis in his body or his environment. It shows that when man turns his attention away from that which terrifies him and steadily contemplates a power that transcends him, something begins to happen that could not happen until his thought is lifted to its highest possible level.

When we treat for a condition we turn steadfastly away

from all the discouraging features, all the ugliness, distortion, misery, and hopelessness. We turn to the highest possible thought of which we are capable, to something that carries a sense of a Power which has never been defeated, to something which creates within us a mental attitude similar to that which the words "The salvation of the Lord" must have carried to those ancient people. Since man's healing is the reflection of his thought, it would seem reasonable that the higher the quality of the thought, the higher would be the manifestation which follows. Whether it can be explained or not at this stage of man's understanding of it, the fact remains that apparent miracles have been wrought by those who have so set their minds.

Dr. Carrel told of seeing deadly conditions healed at Lourdes. Of this he says "The only condition which seems indispensable is prayer." Prayer is a tying in with something Eternal, by whatever name we call It or Him.

ITS QUIET ASSURANCE

This Power that heals is not something spooky, connected with crystal balls, dim lights, and the burning of incense. It has no connection with mysterious voices, visions, or self-hypnosis. But It definitely does work on certain quiet levels. If we miss those levels we miss It; if we attune ourselves to them we contact It.

This Infinite Power always operates on the level of unhurried peace and quietness, because It is always sure of Itself. Unsure man, jittery and tense, is automatically out of touch with It; not that It deliberately withholds Itself, but only those things that are in tune can truly unite. It cannot change to meet man's negative states; man must change to meet Its unchangeable nature. When he "stands still," inwardly as well as outwardly, he places himself in agreement with It and thus comes to see "the salvation of the Lord."

ITS SUFFICIENCY

Nothing in the universe can impose itself upon this Power, for It is completely self-sufficient; therefore, it logically follows that It never finds it necessary to harbor resentment, grudge, hostility, or hate.

Any of these states entertained by man has a tendency to block Its action through him. Thus the Golden Rule is a most practical admonition even from the standpoint of self-interest. Kindliness toward others, absence of criticism, refusal to whisper gossip that would hurt another tend to unite men with Power.

Man is an extension of the Infinite, as the inlet is an extension of the ocean; therefore, that which is true of It must of necessity be true of him. When one comes to realize this, fear of others passes away, and with it the resentment and other negatives, because in his newly realized sufficiency he knows that no one but himself can ever harm him in any way, and that no power on earth can impose itself upon him without his consent.

ITS RESISTLESS EXPRESSION

This Power never sees Itself confronted by any hostile, opposing force. It doesn't expect to see it. It is filled with the concept of Its own Omnipotence; therefore, It knows that nothing can ever keep Its desires from fruition. Man constantly sees barriers and obstructions between him and his desire. This is ungodliness, for the only ungodliness is thinking unlike God thinks. It blocks Power. The correction of this false sense of barrier automatically brings man into tune with Power.

WHAT IS THIS POWER THAT HEALS?

We started out to try to discover what this Power is that heals. We are not sure that anyone knows for certain what it is, but we have endeavored to set up a valid working hypothesis through which one may draw that mysterious Power into his affairs.

We do not think it matters whether we use the personal or the impersonal pronoun in referring to It, because Personality on so vast a scale is impossible of comprehension by our finite minds. We prefer the impersonal because to most persons the personal immediately calls up the image of beard, face, robe, and shepherd's crook. We prefer to think of God as formless, faceless, invisible, intangible, indestructible, abstract Intelligence and Power, intimately connected with the whole universe including man.

This Power directs and works always according to laws of order, harmony, and wholeness which our scientists report finding throughout the material universe. This view of God heals man.

A SUGGESTION ON WHICH TO BUILD PRAYER TREATMENT FOR YOURSELF AND OTHERS

I sense the Presence of the Power that heals, Infinite Wisdom, God.

It is operating in and through us now. It is bringing spiritual understanding, opening up the soul to that which is always seeking man, melting out the false beliefs that have overlaid our spiritual center, dissolving off the film that has kept it from shining through, bringing a sense of our own manhood or womanhood.

Our false belief in that which brings illness is healed. The Power that heals moves through the entire body, filling each cell from the outermost to the innermost, reproducing its own perfection.

In our business lives—our work, our finances—it brings together those who have services to give and those who need those services.

In our personal lives, the Power that heals is touching with its magic fingers to straighten and beautify and make whole wherever needed, guiding and directing and enriching our entire lives.

I release this my thought, declaring that it is so.

There is a Power in man that can lift him toward his highest aspirations and make him the person he wants to be.

No enslavement can hold a person, no illness can defeat him, no problem is insoluble, when he comes to understand the tremendous Power that lies within him just waiting to be released.

Your Emotions Can Kill or Cure

SCIENTIFIC UNDERSTANDING of illness has changed tremendously within the past half century. Two fallacies have been discarded. On the one hand, man has come to see that sickness is not something laid upon him by a Divine Disciplinarian in punishment for sin or in order to strengthen his character. On the other hand, medical science has come to see that many of man's illnesses originate in the emotions and that man's body and his thought are a unit, one and indivisible.

It is daily becoming clearer that man is more than an aggregate of separate organs, one of which can be treated by a heart specialist and another by a stomach specialist without reference to the whole man. This is perhaps more evident in relation to the skin, for the skin specialist in particular is finding an extremely close connection between locked-up personalities and skin eruptions. The trend today is toward treating the "organism as a whole" instead of its separate parts.

CLINICAL EVIDENCE OF LINK BETWEEN EMOTIONS AND HEALTH

TWENTY-FIVE YEARS ago, it was noticed that children reared in public institutions seemed to lack the "will to live" that was possessed by children reared in the family home, and that their death rate was higher. This was brushed aside with the comment that institutions did not give the quality of food and care which the average home did.

But now Dr. Rene A. Spitz, one of the nation's leading psychiatrists, has brought proof of the need for love in the emotional life of the child. He told of a certain foundling home in which ninety-one children were given the best hygienic and nutritional care, but no affection. Within two years, 37 percent of them had died of various diseases.

On the contrary, Dr. Spitz pointed out that in another foundling home, where the physicians, nurses, and visitors were instructed to play with the babies, the children remained practically free of disease. Love and affection seem to provide a defensive force against invading bacteria. Of course, it is also quite evident that the child in the ordinary home becomes ill, even when receiving affection from the parents. But this affection is often accompanied by negative mental states in the parents, such as fear, anxiety, and over-solicitude or "smother love."

Dr. Robinson of Johns Hopkins Hospital studied fifty ulcer patients and found that only six had a real physical basis for this stomach condition. The others were due to emotional causes. Dr. Flanders Dunbar tells of studies made of fifteen hundred admissions to Columbia Presbyterian Medical Center, New York, each with a physical illness correctly diagnosed by a competent physician. Of these it was found that in six hundred physically ill persons, the trouble originated in the emotions. Ninety-two percent of the patients suffering from colitis admitted to Massachusetts General Hospital, Boston, were found to have a long history of continued worry and other emotional strain. When these patients are taught how to rise above worry and anxiety, they show remarkable recovery, with little or no medication.

It is now being shown that a very high proportion of the various heart disorders are decidedly "psychosomatic" in origin. This term is used to describe conditions whose origin is in the "psyche" or mental area and whose manifestation is in the "soma" or body. There are some instances of heart injury during an accident, but many physicians are not so sure whether the actual lesion has come from the physical violence or the emotional shock of the accident.

In other forms of heart trouble, Dr. Flanders Dunbar has gone so far as to "type" the cases. Dr. Dunbar says that persons of certain mental and emotional makeup tend to develop particular sorts of heart trouble. According to these findings, the person who develops coronary occlusion is very likely to be the person in the higher earning brackets. He is a trained or educated person, highly ambitious, conscientious, who is galled by mediocrity, who forces his way toward the top through sheer merit, who has a highly developed sense of responsibility for the support of those dependent upon him, and who drives himself in order to provide it. He is not afraid of competition, but welcomes it.

The angina pectoris type is somewhat similar, except that as a rule he seeks a less competitive field. Perhaps he is not quite so much a fighter as the coronary type.

The irregular-heart type has been classified as "a child afraid of the dark." Perhaps the fears are vague and unnamed, more on the order of a chronic anxiety.

The "rheumatic heart," which might eventually prove to be a misnomer, shows up in the person classified as the "prima donna" type. He is the highly sensitive person who takes offense at things which others would pass by, who flounces out of the room in high dudgeon, who likes to be a big toad in a small puddle, and who dreads nothing so much as having his ego deflated. "But does not the rheumatic heart come from rheumatism?" Yes! But another individual who does not have these particular emotional responses to life seems to be immune to the same physical conditions if he is placed in them.

Scientific delving into personalities has brought forth the fact that arthritis, which is just about as physical a condition as one could have, is in many cases directly traceable to thwarted ambition or disturbed emotions. In fact, the close connection between emotions and illness is becoming so well established that a recent copy of *Kiplinger's Magazine* carried an article entitled, "Does Your Mind Make You Sick?" It then goes on to cite instances in which conditions of an unquestioned physical nature were traced by understanding physicians to their emotional source and recovery was effected.

In one instance, a man, son of a successful father, had taken his own capital to another city and started in business. He was not a good businessman; he failed. He shrank from the idea of returning to his father and of being subjected to the latter's scorn. Soon he developed arthritis. No treatment helped until a far-sighted doctor found the emotional cause.

Recent medical annals are filled with recoveries from such conditions when the patient is taught to understand how they have their origin.

The treatment in this case is not revealed. It could quite easily have been that the doctor pointed out that the patient was not the business type. He might have been extremely artistic, or have had musical proficiency, or have had writing ability. There was no disgrace, therefore, because he had failed in business. Every one of us can do something better than anyone else can, because of our peculiar blend of inherited characteristics and our special training. His father might have signally failed in some activity in which the son was famous. Therefore, with the removal of the sense of shame and self-condemnation, or the fear of his father's condemnation, and the bolstering of his own feelings of adequacy and sufficiency to the point where he was no longer in a state of emotional turmoil, it is quite easy to see how his new mental state could become reflected in his physical organism.

The magazine article cited another instance, that of a very successful man in his middle thirties who enjoyed good health but was greatly disturbed whenever he was assigned to take a business trip to another city some distance away. This emotional disturbance showed itself in a variety of physical symptoms of a distressing nature and finally developed into a genuine heart condition. His physician discovered that the symptoms subsided after the trip had been made. This was the key to the problem.

It seems that several years previously the young man had been sent on an important business trip to this particular city, had dismally failed in his mission, and had become extremely distressed at his failure. Now, whenever he received orders to go out again, the memory of his previous failure and its accompanying pain revived. Buried in the deeper levels of his emotional mind during his active business days, it had gradually faded in memory, as unpleasant experiences tend to do. But with the revival of the memory came the revival of the pain. Because he was too conscientious a worker to object to going on the trip, the repressed emotion had to find outlet somewhere; so it chose some organ of his body through which to express.

Life must express, and particularly the emotional side of life. Civilized man, inhibiting his emotions, builds up a "head of steam" that has to blow through a safety valve. Since man is not exceptionally well equipped with safety valves, the internal pressure finds some organ through which it can "blow off." The result—an illness which is physical in expression but emotional in origin. Fortunately, this young man received understanding assistance, and recovery followed.

All of us pass through extremely painful emotional experiences at some time during our lives. Dr. Flanders Dunbar calls them "delayed mines" which sooner or later explode in illness. A person sometimes feels hopeless because he knows that memory is real and that one can not forget experiences through which he has passed. But one does not have to forget the experience; he only has to learn how to dissociate the pain or the shame from the experience and to reassociate some more pleasant reaction.

THE EMOTIONALLY ADULT ATTITUDE

THE LOSS OF A good job is something final. Not much can be done about it except remember it. But one can search diligently until he finds something that makes that apparent loss bearable. When one realizes that loss is constant in the universe, that separation and reunion are basic in the physical chemistry of the planet, and that every tearing apart is for the purpose of reunion on a different, usually a higher, level, he ceases to bemoan his loss. He takes a constructive view, trying to build the conviction that there is a new union on a higher level for which the separation was necessary. In a short essay, it is not possible to go into this at length, but we are hinting at the constructive way of facing what we erroneously call loss.

The loss of a loved one is also final; yet each of us is a complete unit in himself or herself. Some of us never find it out until death has separated us from a loved one. Knowing the transitory nature of anything physical, the wise person never places his happiness in earthly person, place, or thing. He enjoys it to the full but always retains the sense of his own completeness.

The fullest happiness comes from the complete unit voluntarily joining himself with another complete unit, as every cell of the body unites with its adjoining complete cell, each adding to the fulfillment of the other. Thus one cell may be destroyed without killing the body. In fact, the healthiest form of government is that one in which each citizen, standing independently on his own feet and making his own way, unites with others of like outlook. Each adds to the other's completeness, whereas in any system of parasitism, each weakens the other, himself, and the nation.

One of the most valuable lessons one can learn is that he was made to stand on his own feet and that nature has endowed him with the necessary equipment to do so, but that as soon as he has accepted this responsibility for himself, he finds something else pouring into his life from unseen directions. For life is that way; it demands that we stand alone, then sees that we are never alone.

No one can ever pour into another's experience any more than that person himself can draw. Emerson said that if all the good in the universe were poured over a man, all he could have of it would be that which became his by the right of consciousness. Others may furnish letters of introduction and wish us well, but we are on our own when it comes to making the sale or filling the job adequately.

This is likewise true in regard to our emotions and health. No one but ourselves can draw inner peace and the integration of our inner selves. Doctor or friend may point out the cause of the problem, but man walks in his own path and no one else can enter it, for it is the path of his inner creative center, his own thought.

When a person realizes this, he becomes sturdy and vigorous. He becomes an individual in the truest sense of the word, for having made his choice to stand alone, he moves on to that richest experience, of finding something from beyond man flowing into him.

These newer currents of life can be sanctified by giving them a religious significance, or they can be kept on a level of mental explanation; it is a matter of choice.

I prefer to believe that something greater than man enters into the picture and that he is able to contact the spiritual forces flowing from whatever Intelligence built both him and the universe. I find it hard to believe that the Wisdom that built two fused reproductive cells into an intelligently functioning baby should then lose all interest in it. But I also find it unreasonable to believe that this Intelligence will continue to treat him as a foetus. He is now a reasoning thinker, possessed of the power of choice; therefore, he is evidently intended to use that intelligence to choose which way he will go in life. He must assume the responsibility of an adult and be willing to stand in the power of his own thought.

This emotionally adult attitude is the key to his restoration. It is the coupling that fastens him to the Source of a Power far and away beyond that of the human will. It makes him put away childish attitudes, tantrums, fears, and hatreds and accept the fact that he is on his own, completely adequate to meet life as it comes toward him, self-sufficient with all the resourcefulness of life by virtue of the fact that he is continuously united with greater than human power.

This Power is God in the simplest, nontheological understanding of the term. The person who has thus established a suitable relationship to his Source is thereby held in the grip of an idea which of itself has a stabilizing effect, and which tends to reestablish the inner harmony which is the forerunner of physical well-being.

SECURITY—THE BASIC NEED

ANALYSIS OF THE various emotional states which cause illness or failure in business, in love, or in human relationships leads to the conclusion that insecurity in some form is the basic emotion. Insecurity seems to be the basic "parent-thought" out of which are born such negatives as fear, worry, hate, suspicion, jealousy, envy, and anxiety, as well as many more. Above all else man needs to feel secure. He marries for some external cause, but the basic reason is that he needs someone with whom he can feel secure out of the millions with whom he comes in contact during a lifetime. He thinks he battles for higher wages or larger profits; in reality he battles for security. He thinks he wants the approbation of others; he wants to feel secure in their opinion.

The ill person is never secure; he is not sure that he can eat everything without upsetting himself; he is not sure of his physical ability to carry on his work or to perform other physical activities; if he cannot work, his financial security is endangered; illness threatens the ultimate security called life itself. Health and security are the Siamese twins which must go together. Thus, the expression is often heard, "Well, so long as I have my health, I'm not so bad off. This is the greatest blessing. I can always make more money." Thus man expresses the human hunger for security.

Too often man has misjudged his deepest desire. He has thought that all his efforts were to be directed toward health, money, power, or love. In reality these were only the tokens or the means through which his hunger for security was to be satisfied. The Kingdom of Heaven is this quiet assurance of security. A wise teacher knew that this comes first; he said "Seek ye first the Kingdom [this sense of security] and all these things [wealth, food, etc.] shall be added unto you." Security is the root of which these are the fruit.

Jesus was not so much a religionist as he was a keen observer of life and its hidden sources. He constantly expounded principles which lie beneath actions. He taught men to go beneath the surface of "things" to the hidden roots from which things come. He taught, as moden psychiatry teaches, that man's difficulties lie within himself rather than in the actions of others and that most of man's difficulties with others are precipitated within his own restless, undisciplined self. He taught that the development of a quiet, secure mind is the surest guarantee of outward progress, for it is the magnet which automatically attracts toward a person those "things" for which all humans hunger.

THE BASIS OF SECURITY

But at one point he went further than the modern scientist is permitted to go. The Science of Mind parts company with the psychiatrist and goes with this great Teacher at this point. And this point of departure is perhaps the secret of the tremendous healing influence that this philosophy plays in the physical body.

He pointed out that great illimitable reaches, of which most men are but dimly aware, stretch out into the eternity that is all about us; that man is unconsciously in contact with an Intelligence and a Wisdom so vast and all-embracing that human intelligence is only a drop in the bucket compared to it. He depicted this Intelligence as Omniscient, Omnipotent, and Omnipresent. It contains all the knowledge there is or ever will be, and all of it is present at any point where any of it is.

This is not theological; it is scientific. It has nothing to do with creeds or denominations; it is that which the scientist is trying to say in terms less blunt than we are using. But it is not the province of the scientist to talk of "God" or "the power of God." By the very standards of his profession, he must stop short of defining God or his attributes. He may say: "My studies and research make it plain to me that there is an Intelligence manifested throughout the entire universe. What or who it is I am not prepared to say. But I know that Something is here."

The philosophers of ancient Athens were confronted with the same difficulty. Aware of something they could not define, they set up an altar to "The Unkown God." The man responsible for the spread of Christianity into Europe, one of the best minds of that or any day, was not deterred by their agnosticism. Paul said, "This god whom ye worship without defining, him I declare unto you; he is not far from any one of us, for in him we live, move, and have our being."

Modern man is like a blind child groping in the dark. He needs security most of all. He senses that there is something to which he can tie, which can give him the anchorage for which his soul, heart, mind, and emotions hunger. His inability to contact it brings about this horrible sense of insecurity; this leads him into a state of inner conflict, with its resultant frustrations, inner rages, and complexes. Thoughts are things. It is impossible for them to stay forever locked within; they, like murder, will out.

Sweeping in brain waves throughout his entire body, in wave after wave, eventually they reproduce themselves in their distinctive patterns. The tissues gradually take on the characteristics of the pattern. The doctor calls it arthritis, ulcer, high blood pressure, heart trouble, or something else. These are only physical names for emotional outlets. Healing comes when the inner man is healed. Otherwise it is useless to doctor the effect.

Each person's inner pattern is different from all others, for it is himself in his individual reaction to life. One finds himself with less ambition, lowered vitality, unclear thinking, muddled and confused. He makes a mistake and thinks it is because he is confused, but he is confused because he is insecure. No man is big enough to tie himself onto himself. He must tie to something vastly bigger, something with limitless potential. Man is insecure because he is separated; he needs that clear understanding of unity, reunion, restoration of contact with his Source.

This great Teacher showed this when he told a simple story about a prodigal son. Foolish interpreters have thought this story was a warning against loose morals; it was a piece of the loftiest teaching ever given to mankind. The son had everything as long as he remained in the father's house, which means union with his source. But wandering into a far country, he found nothing but misery; this grew out of insecurity. He regained both security and inner harmony when he made his way back to "the Father's house."

No one ever taught this principle better than Jesus did. He found his fellow-men in misery, resigned to its inevitability in a dull, apathetic manner, or else blaming someone else for their woes. He showed them the only solution to their problems; a few saw it and took it.

One difficulty is that whenever Jesus is mentioned, the average man becomes uncomfortable. The name has an otherworldly, holy connotation, because he is usually associated in our minds with a cross, a creed, ritual, dogma, and sanctimoniousness.

Jesus was first and foremost a practical man. He knew that one's emotions can kill or cure, pauperize or make prosperous, keep him in turmoil or bring him peace. He knew that man is not a body containing an elusive something called a soul but that he is a mind inhabiting a body and master of all that body's experiences. He knew that man is the invisible person with a temporary body in which he lives for the time he is on this physical earth and which enables him to get around upon it. He knew that when man understands himself from this point of view, he becomes the arbiter of his own destiny.

Jesus seemed astounded that man could be so blind to his real nature and potentialities. He found people groping, crying, and pleading for freedom from their bondage. He said: "It's all within yourself. Both cause and effect are within you. The link between them is within you. The power to change your conditions is within you. The entire kingdom of heaven is within you. There is no need to look anywhere outside of yourself for the alteration, for there is no external emancipator."

He tried to show them how to make the necessary alterations in their thinking. He tried to take their attention away from the magnitude of their difficulties to the greater magnitude of the healing power that already lay within them. He portrayed an Infinite Healing Presence which operates through every natural law, yet above it. He let them know that this powerful Presence is able to triumph over any condition, no matter how apparently hopeless.

Then he brought forth the connection that would link them to this healing power; that link is faith. Constantly he stressed this matter of faith, the connecting link between man and his desires, between man and God. His constant reiteration was "It is done unto you as ye believe"; "Your faith will save you"; "Here is irresistible power, and over there is your great need. Can you believe that this power can flow through that serious situation and heal it? If you can, you will be healed; if you believe not, you shall die in your sin [blindness]."

THE WAY INTO SECURITY

JESUS TAUGHT LITTLE of the life beyond; in fact his teaching upon this subject is not too clear. But with the utmost clarity he pointed out the way into heaven while on earth. He did not try to set up a theological system, nor to hold people to a creed. He taught life and how to live it. He knew that man continues after death very much the same as he is here. Those who have a hunger for spiritual knowledge will continue to grow and expand in that knowledge. Those who have attained a certain amount of mastery of mental law here will be more at home in that extended phase of living in which mental law is the only law. He knew that the afterlife is continuous with the present, the only difference being that it is lived on a non-physical plane.

The spiritual view of life enables man to live here as he will live there, seeing spiritual things as the true reality and the earthly things as their shadows. A person living from this vantage point needs no prohibitions, for within himself he will sense that which is contrary to the universe and will govern himself accordingly.

The person who lives primarily in the body, or from the material point of view, thinks wickedness consists in actions. Jesus taught that it lies in the thought. The ancient Hebraic teaching consisted chiefly in "Thou shalt nots," for their laws were laid down while they were an undisciplined aggregation of newly released slaves, wandering the wilderness after their release from soul-deadening Egyptian bondage. It is not easy to teach such a handicapped people the deeper principles; that would come later in their history. At the moment, it was sufficient to warn them that if any of them were caught violating the "Thou shalt nots," punishment would follow.

Jesus taught that sin lies in the thought. He said "You have been taught of olden times, 'Thou shalt not commit adultery,' but I say that whosoever looketh upon a woman to lust after her hath already committed adultery with her in his heart." And, "Ye have heard of olden times, 'Thou shalt not kill,' but I say that whosoever hateth his brother is a murderer." Thus he pointed the way to the true place of causation, within the thought.

Many persons refrain from the overt act but are making themselves ill by the quality of their inner thought. Thus

Swedenborg stated a scientific as well as a psychiatric thought when he said, "The angels read man's autobiography in his structure." The word "sin" means a state of dim vision which causes a man to miss the implications of his actions. Jesus showed that the sin is the inner blindness rather than the outer act. Failure is not in the act, but in the thought. A man's inner self goes broke long before his business does. One's moral fiber weakens within him long before the world sees it in his actions. Illness starts long before a physician can diagnose it from the physical signs and symptoms.

So, in setting our emotions on the side of healing, it might not be so old-fashioned to take the way that this great Teacher outlined. Instead of "Thou shalt not kill," he stated positively, "Thou shalt love thy neighbor as thyself." Instead of saying "An eye for an eye," he said, "Love thine enemies, and bless them that persecute you."

His was a positive philosophy of life, based upon the fact that as one enters the Kingdom, he leaves the old laws of the world of tooth and claw behind and finds himself operating in spiritual law, which is more potent than natural law, and which sometimes seems to be diametrically opposed to it.

The man who is reluctant to let go of the old natural law of hurting those who hurt us binds himself thereby to the earthy; therefore the earth laws of health become his master. He who moves to the new level frees himself from the laws that lay others aside ill; these do not have the same power over him as over them. Thus we find a far smaller percentage of illness among those who understand this philosophy of life.

In practice, "loving thy neighbor" works like this: When someone appears to be the enemy, we move toward the center of life into the quiet place which exists within every one of us, detaching ourselves as far as possible from their hostility, so that there is not the urge to return tit for tat. We try to understand why they hold hostility toward us, or why they are trying to undermine us.

Most of our quarrels with others arise because we think they are wrong; on the other hand, they think we are wrong. Yet in every person is an urge to do the right thing. Some of us may have been taught from childhood that the smart thing is to take advantage of others, consoling ourselves with the idea that it is their business to look out for themselves and believing that if others had the chance, they would take advantage of us. These persons think this is the right way to live, for they regard the world as a "dog eat dog" sort of place. The understanding person sees their point of view and, while taking every possible step to keep from being imposed upon, nevertheless remains free from censoriousness.

Each nation is always trying to do the best it can for itself. Each class in society, each group, each individual is always trying to do the best. Because of partial blindness, a person or a group does not always see the end result of that which it sets in motion. This is not necessarily badness; it is ignorance. His action might result in hurt to us, but if we descend to his level and try to get even, we have merely added fuel to the fire of ignorance. At his death, Jesus did not berate his murderers nor hate them. He did not say they were bad. He merely said, "They know not what they do."

This is not nearly so impractical a system as some would think who have followed the old law of getting even, for the person who does this eventually comes to radiate an atmosphere which in some mysterious way draws what he wants instead of what he doesn't want. Life becomes quieter; the principle of harmony thus set up at a man's center begins to draw the more harmonious elements into his environment.

His body, even his business, comes to show this same characteristic in various unexpected forms.

A law of the universe demands that if one brings sorrow into the life of another, sometime, somewhere, someone will bring sorrow into that one's life. On the other hand, if we determine that we shall bring the good into the lives of others, this same law will demand that sometime, somewhere, someone will bring the good into our lives. This is all that Paul meant when he said, "Love is the fulfilling of the law."

This attitude of unfailing goodwill toward others is in itself a healing force. It is not merely a vaporous emotion that makes one feel good while expressing it. It is an actual force, and it has terrific healing impact upon the person exercising it. It is most practical in spite of anything the semi-blind person says.

It is well if we can study and learn the actual techniques of treating illness in this way. But all the study is useless if love is absent; whereas the person lacking in technique but whose heart enfolds those he meets is already on his way to becoming a healer of men.

Naturally, this is a high ideal. None of us lives up to it completely; yet it holds the key to getting along with nations, classes, groups, family, business associates, and, finally, with our own most difficult selves. The person who is at war with someone else was first at war with himself. He who comes to be at peace with himself is soon at peace with others. As we let the bitterness drop away, the rancor fade, the envy and jealousy be replaced by friendliness, we enter a new world, in which it will soon become clearly evident that our emotions can cure us where before they sought to kill us.

A SUGGESTED TREATMENT

A VERY GENERAL outline for treatment follows. Go quietly by yourself and say:

No one is in competition with me to take away anything that is mine. My job, my customers, my loved ones, my reputation, my success are all mine by right of consciousness. No one can possibly take from me that which is rightfully mine, even as I do not desire to take from anyone that which is rightfully his.

All men seek their own, as I do mine. This Infinite Law now draws my own good to me through union with the Source of all there is; therefore I rest quietly. I allow the turbulence to die away. I absorb myself in the thought of Infinite Peace and quietness. I now believe that God touches me at the center of my being. I accept that touch, for from it my own quietness arises.

This word that I now speak reverses the direction of my past thought. I let all the negative and destructive currents go by, for my thought now is directed only toward that which is positive and constructive. I confidently look toward the manifestation of my new thought-trend in better health, better business, better relations with all with whom I am thrown in contact. I bless them and wish for them the same peace that is mine, the same growth and expansion.

I try not to make this complicated. I keep it simple, merely trying to entertain the attitudes I think the Infinite must hold, one of which is goodwill toward men. I think of all men as my friends and cooperators and myself as their cooperator.

I now speak this word, declaring that the One Infinite Healing Presence operates perfectly in me. Nothing destruc-

tive can work within me, for only the perfect pattern of life can reproduce itself in and through my body. I release my belief in the power of anything to hold me without my consent. I declare my entire freedom, mental and physical, at this moment and through all the coming years. And it IS *so!*

Help Answer Your Own Prayers

MAN HAS MORE unfulfilled desires than any other creature that walks the earth. He is forever held in the grip of desires that seem to be just beyond his reach. The animals have a few desires, most of which are attainable. They seem to be satisfied with what they get, but when they are placed in the laboratory and thrown into conflict with themselves in order to test their reactions, they develop nervous breakdowns and the various neuroses that afflict the human race. Left alone in his native habitat, the animal has no neurosis. He lives his life. He accepts what is. He goes hungry at times and is glutted at other times, but he seems to live on a fairly steady emotional level.

It is the mark of the divine in man that he shall forever be filled with the "Divine Discontent." It is that which separates him from the animal; this is why no animal ever prays, and no man lives who does not pray.

The most primitive tribes that have been found anywhere, however limited their vocabulary, always have a word for God; this is man's answer to the incessant hunger for something just beyond his reach.

No matter what laws would be passed against prayer, they never would be observed. Those who make the laws would in times of crisis find themselves instinctively praying even while trying to enforce the law, for prayer is an integral part of human nature. It never can be eradicated, because prayer is more than man's outreaching for the Infinite. It is the hunger of the Infinite for a more complete and perfect expression in and through man, and in one sense it is the voice of God speaking through our lips.

From time immemorial man has prayed, and it is interesting to note the progression that has occurred in the concept of prayer. At one time he prayed to or against the elements; the thunder and the lightning were to him his God. And then he began to conceive of incorporeal entities floating about in the air, surrounding him, blocking or helping him; so he began to pray to these in order to placate them or to gain their assistance.

Later, prayer became more of a personal thing. Man began to conceive of God, first of all, as a divine Autocrat in the heavens. Later still, He was thought of as a Law Giver, who set laws out by which man should live, and still later as a stern Judge to inflict penalties for the infraction of those laws. The idea grew into that of a King, sometimes mellow and handing out blessings, sometimes driven by His anger at man's disobedience, then to that of a Shepherd—"The Lord is my shepherd"—looking after the sheep, and then ultimately, in the time of Jesus, as our Father, although Hebrew prophets had held this concept also. It is our belief that the inner attitude, rather than the form of address, determines the certainty of the answer; too many prayers of all types have been answered for us ever to say that any man's method of prayer is not right.

But as we come into this modern age, man prays to something less physical than that anthropomorphic type of God. Man recognizes that God is Light, Life, Love, Wisdom, and Power in an impersonal sense, yet becoming warmly personal to the individual who sees the connection of himself with this infinite Light, Life, Love, Wisdom, and Power.

Consequently, in the Science of Mind we do not use the forms which some of us used in years gone by. We come to recognize that prayer is an attitude of mind rather than a series of words spoken. We come to believe that man is the extension of the Infinite Mind and that whatever is true of that Mind is basically true of him. Of course, man doesn't always live up to that which is true of him. But when the Bible says, "Be ye perfect as your Father in heaven is perfect," it is not merely a command impossible to fulfill. It is a statement of basic truth, for a man at the divine center of his being is just as spiritually perfect as the Infinite is.

This is the difference between what we call "being" and "becoming." That which we desire is what we basically are. We desire perfection. We want a higher level of living tomorrow than we have today. We want a greater degree of understanding than we now have. We want progression in our material and physical affairs. The mere fact that man hungers for this is an evidence that somewhere within him there is that perfect norm which is without spot, limitation, hindrance, or pain anywhere; and his cry for it is his spoken response to that which already is stirring within him.

Our prayer, therefore, is the outgoing of our deeper selves to that which gently nudges us from within.

Perhaps the best-known prayer in the civilized world is what is known as "The Lord's Prayer." We find it in the sixth chapter of the book of Matthew, beginning at verse six. It runs something like this, beginning with a kind of introduction:

"But thou, when thou prayest, enter into thy closet, and when thou hast shut thy door, pray to thy Father who is in secret; and thy Father who seeth in secret shall reward thee openly.

"And use not vain repetitions, as the heathen do: for they think that they shall be heard for their much speaking.

"But pray ye after this manner:

"Our Father who art in heaven, hallowed be thy name.

Thy Kingdom come. Thy will be done in earth as it is in heaven."

The next verse says, "Give us," but scholars say that the proper interpretation is "Thou givest us each day our daily bread. Thou forgivest us our trespasses as we forgive those who trespass against us.

"Thou leadest us not into temptation, or testing, but thou deliverest us from evil: For thine is the kingdom, and the power, and the glory forever. Amen."

Now, that prayer is rattled off thoughtlessly by millions of people every Sunday morning in services, yet it is a beautiful prayer. It is just about as perfect a circle of prayer as one could imagine, because it has seven phrases in it, or seven distinctions. Seven is usually accounted the perfect number in the Bible.

ANALYSIS OF "THE LORD'S PRAYER"

"Our Father who art in heaven . . ."

THIS PRAYER STARTS out by trying to evoke a state of mind, to build a mood or a consciousness at the beginning which will color and give meaning to all that follows. Thus, it starts with "Our Father who art in heaven." Heaven in the Bible is not necessarily a place beyond the sky. Heaven always is representative of the perfect state of consciousness, just as earth always represents the physical affairs of an individual.

Man inherits along two lines: the line of his physical progenitors from whom he gets the color of his eyes and his bodily build and all of his physical characteristics; but man likewise inherits along a spiritual line, in which he inherits a spiritual nature and a spiritual center, something deep within which is "heaven," while the body is "earth."

Jesus seemed to be endeavoring to set forth before those people that the thing or person they are praying to is that perfect state, the Unconditioned Awareness of Being, that which is not influenced by any of the vicissitudes of life, that which stays steady like the shining sun. Clouds may rise out of the earth side of man's nature and hide this shining sun, but he who knows that the sun is there is not too upset over these temporary cloudings within himself. He learns to say, "In spite of all these things I do that I don't want to do, I know that there is the Father in me existing always in heaven, the perfect state of consciousness."

"Hallowed be thy name"

And then the prayer goes on to say, "Hallowed be thy name." The name usually indicates the nature. *Hallowed* is a very peculiar word. It is more than "holy." It is more than "whole." It is more than "healing," and yet they are all relative to this term. *Hallowed* carries the impression of a spotless purity which is so far beyond the finest that we could imagine as to be otherworldly. It conveys the picture of a great field covered with snow upon which not one particle of soot has ever fallen, the transcendent beauty of that spreading snowfield as seen on the farms of the Middle West, where that spotlessly white blanket silently lies, upon which no animal has walked. There is not a single footprint; not even the claws of a bird have touched it. Nothing there but unviolated purity. The perfect Absolute, the Hallowed!

Since man's answers to prayer are the reflection of the level of his thought, it naturally follows that if our thought is mingled with the "dirt of the earth," our answers will correspond. But if we can raise our thought to a higher level, one in which we deliberately cultivate more kindliness, it still may not be spotless, but it will be a higher quality. Our prayer will be correspondingly effective, because our inward states determine its effectiveness.

If in some way we can detach ourselves from all that is ugly anywhere in life, and if, thinking of these spotless fields of snow, we can bring ourselves to the realization that this is the nature of the Infinite, then we shall have grasped the meaning of *hallowed.* It is more than "holy" and more than "whole." It is a spotlessness that is above any possibility of defilement. Then that picture which we are able to engender within ourselves reflects itself back to us and, thus reflecting, it begins to produce in us something of the nature of that which we contemplate.

Unquestionably Jesus raised the consciousness of prayer to a very high level. And when we sometimes hear a congregation thoughtlessly racing through "Our Father who art in heaven, hallowed be thy name," it shocks us by its sacrilege. We are not against the Lord's Prayer by congregations, but how much people would be enriched spiritually if they could get the meaning of the various phrases as they must have been in the mind of that great Teacher when he laid out before them this ideal of the absolute perfection which lies within them as the Father who is in "the heaven," or the heavenly state, the highest state of consciousness.

"Thy kingdom come, Thy will be done . . ."

Then Jesus says, "Thy will be done in earth as it is in heaven." This is where it becomes practical. In the high state of consciousness there is no blocking of the eternal will. The will of the Infinite is always the reproduction in man of what the Infinite is in Himself; therefore, thy will be done in "me, the earth" as it is in "thee, the heaven," the exalted, the hallowed, consciousness.

No healing can ever come from a source lower than itself. Healing must always be the emergence from something which has the qualities and the attributes of perfection. Consequently as we think of the great hallowed, sweeping hills of beautiful snow, and if they speak to us and give us a more vivid idea of the God in us, then we can say "Thy will be done in my earth body as it is in thy heavenly body."

"Give us this day . . ."

Jesus goes on to say, "Thou givest us each day our daily

bread." Here is life. Man cannot live without bread. It is a means of showing that man forever is indissolubly united with this that is hallowed and that it is the pouring of the eternal purity through him which manifests as life, love, wisdom, and supply. The bread that we put into our physical mouths is only at the very end of that picture, because it means that whatever supply we ever have is the great hallowed field of the Infinite pouring itself through us into material form.

That which we call "supply," that is, dollars, business, sales—all these things are highly necessary and very desirable for us to seek; but we must see that he who seeks them only on their external side is missing the whole logical sequence, because supply is spiritual in its origin. The channel through which our supply comes may be cut off suddenly. This concern may go out of business. That customer may pass away or move elsewhere. If we always have our eyes on the daily bread as it comes through a channel, then we are of all men most shaky.

The spiritual thinker would say, "Away back in the heights of that hallowed consciousness supply has flowed to me from the day I was born. The channel through which it flowed has gone out of business. The means by which I was able to earn it are now no more, for I am now aged; but supply never fails. Thou givest me my daily bread." This is a spiritual concept, and even in the active hurly-burly of life the man who is a good businessman from the practical side will be a better businessman when he lays the spiritual foundation. He then sees not just the bread at the end of his material operations; he goes further back and knows himself to be united with the spiritual source of supply. To that degree he is also the originator from his "heaven" side of that which appears on his "earth" side.

When the individual does this, he begins to find something

happening in his life that was not happening before. He finds his business moving along on higher, safer levels; he finds a steadiness and a security to that supply which was never there while he was looking only at the customer, the channel, the agency through which that good would come.

"Forgive us . . ."

"Forgive us our trespasses as we forgive them who trespass against us." Since we are thinking of attitudes which help answer our own prayer, it is well to remember that no one can ever get his healing if his problem comes from a certain attitude which he refuses to give up. Unforgivingness is probably the greatest blocker of answered prayer that there is. No one knew this better than Jesus; therefore, he put it in among those seven qualifications for the good prayer.

The unforgivingness may never be allowed to show itself toward another individual; sometimes it is held within where it may continue to eat away unknown to others. We may have been reared to be polite ladies and gentlemen; therefore, we do not engage in cursing and hating people outwardly and throwing things, but if within we are not forgiving the trespasses of the other individual, then that in itself acts as a block. It is important that we understand this, because the whole problem of humanity today is a refusal to forgive the trespassers.

Russia holds grudges because of what we did to her in 1918. The wars between Germany and France were wars of revenge over Alsace-Lorraine. Some Southern people cannot forget the Civil War. All the time something festers within the individual who refuses to forgive. Within ourselves we find a certain disgruntledness because of what someone has done to us. It is always better if we can rise above it, for it will block the answer to our prayer.

Instead of harboring resentment, we recapture the beautiful snow-covered hills; we think "hallowed is thy name." This unforgivingness is sordid. The "snow" is blackened with "mud" that comes through from the "earth." We turn from its ugliness toward the beauty of forgiveness. How easy it is to forgive men their trespasses when we recognize that this is the hallowed place from which comes the opening of our channels and the bringing to us of that which we want.

"Lead us not into temptation . . ."

"Thou leadest us not into temptation [or testing] but thou deliverest us from evil." Man is always led into his trials by his own lesser self, his earth self, his earth side. By the very nature of life there are certain situations into which we are bound to run between the cradle and the grave. No one of us will ever have the nice easy path that some of us dream of, because other people may be selfish and uncooperative; difficult situations often develop; but the thing to keep in mind is that all of those grow out of the "earth" nature of man, not out of the nature of the universe.

Someone who is passing through deep sorrow sometimes asks, "Is God testing me through this experience?" It is not true that God places us in awkward circumstances in order to test us, that we might learn a lesson. Man's inhumanity to man can test us. We can make it a self-testing. We can decide to learn the lesson out of the experience, but the experience never comes from God; He never leads into temptation to test any man. There is merely the free choice of millions of people in the earth, and out of their free choice come the ugly parts of life. He who lives under the sway of the hallowedness of the high consciousness may turn the trespass of others into a lesson which enables him to surmount, to develop wings, to rise above that which otherwise would bog him down. "Thou deliverest [or separatest] us from evil."

"For thine is the kingdom . . ."

The kingdom—that is the manifestation. In the prayer we say, "Thy kingdom come, thy will be done, in earth as it is in heaven." The kingdom is the recognition by man of that which he truly is, a surrendering to it and the allowing of the hallowedness of that kingdom to come forth and show in his life. He is not responsible for the life of anyone else. He should leave the other person and what he does alone. He should say, "My business is to allow that kingdom to come." That kingdom then will manifest. We cannot repeat too often that it is always the manifestation of the hallowedness of what we call heaven.

"Thy will be done, in earth as it is done in heaven." The will of the Father is never in conflict with itself or with anything else. There are never any cross-purposes within the nature of God, for the Infinite dwells forever in completest harmony, in the hallowedness of "heaven," the perfect state of consciousness.

Our desire is that as it is in "heaven" (God) so shall it be in "earth" (us). There could be a secondary meaning that God's will be done throughout the earth, but the only way this will ever come about is through individuals coming one by one to grasp the inner meaning of this phrase. Thus, from one to another "thy will" can spread throughout the earth. We try too hard to get the other fellow to do God's will. We should concentrate on letting it be done in us.

"And the power." The power is the power of that Creative Mind which brings it. "And the glory." This is the extreme bursting forth into life and into the form of our affairs of the hallowedness of the Infinite. They all are of God.

Man is merely the recipient, the co-worker, the surrender to this which is trying to operate in and through him.

The *Reader's Digest* recently told the story of a man who allowed that thing to happen. He was Lt. Commander Edwin Miller Rosenberg, a navy man. You may have read of this incident. All his life he wanted to be a navy man. He loved the navy. He had a hard time getting an appointment, but he finally got it—to Annapolis; he was graduated just about the time of Pearl Harbor. He had three years' combat service. When his ship was decommissioned, he was sent into a hospital for observation, because he was not feeling well. The physicians discovered a malignant tumor within him and gave him two weeks to live. They told him to get an attorney to draw up his will. His response was, "I believe that I have something to do in life." He believed in prayer and he said, "I'm going to pray this thing through." They had him in and out of the hospital for two or three years. Then they discovered another cancer, this time in his neck, then another in the kidney. They advised him that there was no chance, not the slightest. And he said, "You do the examining, and I'll do the hoping." He continued to pray.

They gave him radiation, saying, "It won't do you much good, but we will give it to you." But he insisted he would pray this thing through. And at thirty-two years of age, the man has prayed himself out of those four malignancies. When his story went abroad, letters came in from people everywhere. What did you do? How did you do it? He said, "I can't teach you to pray. I'll tell you as much as I can of the inner attitude." He said that he who gives up hoping is beaten. The man who continues to hope and to know that there is a Power greater than anything that comes against him—that man has a chance. He said, "Not all those I prayed for lived, but some of them did, and it was the attitude they took that healed them." The attitude was, "Thy perfection be done in my earth body as it is in thy spiritual nature."

Here is the earth form—ugly, distorted, offensive. He turned away from it. This picture evidently filled the doctor's mind; so he said, "You can have that. Let me turn from it to the great hallowed snow fields of the Infinite. If I keep thinking and talking of it, I'm going to be worse." He made a pact with his wife that they would never discuss it except constructively. They were turning back to that hallowed center from which all healing comes, and as a result, at thirty-two years of age this man proved something for himself and is helping other people to find it.

This is what we mean by helping answer our own prayers. The prayers would naturally fulfill themselves but for the fears, the anxieties, or the unforgiveness we harbor toward the trespasser. Everything in the Lord's Prayer is for the purpose of getting man and his little self out of the way and letting operate that which wants to operate in its fullest. When it is given a perfect right of way, then the Almighty healing power of that hallowed hill will move in and through, whether it be a financial condition or a physical, a domestic condition or loneliness, a destructive habit or an ugly disposition, or any condition whatever.

And then "Thine is the kingdom, and the power, and the glory" of the manifestation. Man never takes the credit to himself, for man never answers his own prayer. Man merely makes himself a fit subject for God to answer in and through him when man brings his consciousness up to that which is called "heaven."

Thy will be done in the earth body, in my affairs, as it is done on those hallowed hills of perfect purity, as it is done in the heaven consciousness.

MEDITATION

As we move away from the things of the outer world, we endeavor to think of whatever it is that brings to us this sense of a certain heavenly level—not a theological heaven, but the heaven of man's loftiest consciousness.

As we think of that which has never been violated in any way, that which is as the pure driven snow on a country landscape, we endeavor to absorb the feeling of it and to sense that no matter how far we ever have fallen short, there still is within us that hallowed part of our nature, the God-in-us.

We turn to this, turning away from all those things which are ugly and defiled, which are twisted and warped. We turn to that which in its smooth, gentle undulation speaks to us of something not touched by the hand of man.

We declare now that every person turning inward to that inner center, the hallowed place, is receiving something, is catching something which, spreading out through the layers of his mind or her mind, is altering the attitude not only toward the condition but toward other people and is spreading out through the physical circle of the business, the body, the home, the habits, or anything one is doing on that earth side of life, making it like that which already exists on the heaven side of life.

Quietly now, without forcing or struggling, we surrender ourselves to the perfect working of the Infinite Law of the Creative Mind in and through us. Perfect God, perfect man, perfect structure and function, perfect being, perfect activity, and perfect feeling now are the law of life to every person in this place.

And we release this our word. We know that it isn't by our wrestling with it that the answer comes. We just let it go, and we say that this is the truth about every person in this place whether he believes it or not. It is the truth about him; and as we release it, we give thanks for it, because we know at this moment that it is so.

Is There a Cure for Frustration?

CERTAIN WORDS CAN easily become shelters into which timid souls run when life becomes difficult. *Frustration* is such a word. It has become the refuge of cowards and has taken on a technical significance which obscures its real meaning.

Superficial thinkers confuse frustration with obstacles and difficulties. The latter may set up an attitude of frustration, but in themselves they may be the very thing needed to induce the very reverse. Society has been shocked by so-called "rat-pack" outrages, in which gangs of youths roam the city assaulting citizens who refuse them money. It has been said that these youths are frustrated, because they live in poverty and because they are discriminated against because of their national origin; yet their brothers are on the police force endeavoring to maintain law against these law-breakers.

Evidently, then, frustration indicates one's reaction to the obstacle rather than the obstacle itself. Moreover, for every youth thus ranged against law and order, there are one hundred of his brothers and sisters engaged quietly in productive work, held in high respect by society.

UNFRUSTRATED PEOPLE

It is a striking fact that those who have left great names in history have often been those who had every reason to give up in despair. But they have pushed on in spite of serious impediments. Homer and Milton faced the obstacle of blindness. Helen Keller was also deaf and dumb. Sidney Lanier and Robert L. Stevenson fought lifelong battles with tuberculosis. Handel wrote his great oratorio, *The Messiah*, when paralyzed and in dire poverty. Charles Steinmetz was a misshapen hunchback. Charles E. Potter lost both his legs in the recent war but never lost his fighting spirit. He ran for Congress successfully in Michigan. Charles Lamb stuttered painfully yet supported and cared for his insane sister, refusing to commit her to an asylum. In an early love affair Madame Curie had her heart broken, and she lived in pitiful poverty, but went on to a successful marriage and persisted in her research in a foreign land.

One could use pages reciting such incidents, only to show that life and the "slings and arrows of outrageous fortune" are never, in themselves, sufficient to turn back the person so long as he is possessed of the unconquerable soul. The story of frustration is never what life does to us; it is what we do to life.

SAGA OF THE SOUTHWEST

THE FAMOUS SOUTHWEST Museum in Los Angeles is a monument to a man who never knew the meaning of frustration. Seventy years ago Charles Fletcher Lummis started from Ohio for Los Angeles on foot. He carried fishing tackle but no gun. For five months he walked over dim trails and sometimes no trails, making his living as he went. Across snow-clad mountains and waterless deserts he slowly made his way, narrowly escaping death at the hands of an escaped convict. He fell over a cliff and broke his arm, far from civilization. Making a rough splint and sling, he pushed on. Arriving in the infant city of Los Angeles, he got a job on the *Times*, soon becoming editor. His future looked rosy, but a stroke left him with one arm dangling. Here was the end of the road for one easily turned back. But Lummis believed that every ending is only a beginning; he mapped out a new career.

Soon we find him in New Mexico, living with the Indians, absorbing their atmosphere, learning their language, recording their folklore. He learned to mount a horse, shoot and fish with one usable arm. He drove teams of horses hauling freight. Once when the team bogged down in a roaring flood, he unloaded the heavy freight, carried it to the river bank, whipped and encouraged the horses to budge the wagon, then loaded it all again on the farther side.

Lummis recorded almost a thousand of the haunting melodies which the Spanish and Indians sang, preserving for posterity one of the richest fields of our folklore. Another stroke re-crippled him, but he never was diverted from his goal. With it all, he maintained a remarkable charm and an unfailing sense of humor. When he could no longer walk, he pleaded with his friends to put him on a horse, and he fished from the river banks.

A third stroke put him in the hospital at Santa Fe. The prognosis was bad; it was to be only a matter of time until the end. Instead of writing funereal material, he wrote humor. Recovering, he returned to the Pacific Coast and planned the Southwest Museum. Finally, blindness overtook him, but his soul still saw clearly. He drew the plans for the Museum, creasing the paper instead of drawing lines, and feeling along the creases as he described his plan to the architect. Those who were fortunate enough to be invited to his Pasadena home in his declining years speak of Charles Fletcher Lummis as the personification of the invincible. Never a word of defeat or frustration fell from his lips; always there was the forward-looking attitude of hope and expectancy.

WHAT FRUSTRATION IS

What, then, is frustration? It is an attitude which shrinks from coming to grips with life and which uses outer obstacles as an excuse rather than an adequate reason.

Life is a school. Man is placed in it in order to know himself. Life is a pathway of self-discovery. Man has tremendous inner resources—far more than most of us realize. It is not reasonable to assume that Deity places obstacles in our path in order to test us. This reduces the Infinite to the stature of a magnified human being. But life itself is not easy. We live in a community of human beings, each faulty and selfish as we are. There is bound to be a clash of interests. People will not give us our own way. Our violation of physical law brings physical handicaps upon us, even when we have violated law unwittingly. There are always adequate and sufficient reasons for every physical disability, chief among which is our ignorance of the law of cause and effect. But trials are certainly not "testings" by the Infinite; they are inherent in the process of living. Since we cannot avoid them, the wise person learns how to face them, to take them in stride. The shortsighted man whimpers and complains, feeling sorry for himself. Self-pity is one of the most weakening and deadening attitudes one can develop. It stifles hope and strangles effort. Another Charles Lummis might have ended up with a tin cup on the streets of Los Angeles. That poet knew life who declared that it's the set of sails, and not the gales, which determines whether one ship sails east and another west.

LIFE MUST EXPRESS ITSELF

LIFE IS A SCHOOL of self-expression. Man must express all that he is, or feel frustrated. Life within him is forever thrusting outward. Man does not determine this; Life does. For Life is far more than the feeble pulses of our individual lives. Life is eternal, immeasurable, irresistible, for Life is some form of the Infinite. Life in the absolute sense surges forward and outward continually, for this seems to be its nature. Where It is denied, blocked, or impeded in its outthrust, It turns inward upon Itself. This in-turning is frustration.

Under favorable conditions, Life will always fulfill Itself. Place the seed of tree, animal, or man in favorable conditions for its development, it will come to full term. Growth and expansion are the law of Life.

Why, then, does Life not always complete Itself? Assuming that two persons are faced with similar obstacles, why does one quit while the other goes on? Are some born with more determination than others? Is tenacity unequally imparted to the newborn?

Modern psychologists point out that most of our attitudes are determined during the years of infancy and childhood. They point out that the child born to neurotic or shiftless parents will be thrown into internal conflict early in life. He needs a feeling of security in order to grow normally. His parents are so wrapped up in their own problems that they have no time or inclination to help him with his security problem. They may quarrel much with each other. They may be overprotective of him, never allowing him to develop means of solving his own problems. They may be sharp and cruel one moment, excessively penitent and sentimental the next. The result is that the child gradually comes to feel alone, insecure in a hostile world. In trying to find security, he learns how to find a false sense of security by attaching himself to someone stronger. He then loses his own initiative, spending his life trying to accommodate himself to what others want. He becomes a first-class doormat or "yes" man.

But this theory is suspect because two children from the same family with exactly the same pressures placed upon them will turn out to be quite different. So conditioning is not the complete answer. One brother becomes a gangster, the other a district attorney, from the selfsame home. We must look elsewhere for the cause and cure of frustration.

NO FRUSTRATION FROM BLINDNESS

ONE OF THE MOST popular teachers at South High School in Omaha is Dr. Edward Kuncel. As a child he ran into trees and furniture, hurt himself, picked himself up and went on playing, thinking that everyone did the same, for he did not know that he had been born blind. His father was a man of great physical courage who never babied the son. His mother was an instinctive psychologist who kept Edward's courage and hope high. At five he was sent to a school for the blind, coming home on weekends. There he stayed until he was fifteen. He learned to read Braille and to type, but he heard the other children speaking of their limitations and determined that he would live as if he were normal. He refused the aid of a dog. He would not allow others to lead him. He found his own way to the streetcar, learned to listen for the sounds, knew a certain noise the car made going over an imperfect rail one block before his home, quietly made his way to the door, and alighted at his own corner. Walking on the street, he came to recognize certain unevennesses in the pavement so that he turned in without hesitation at his own gate.

At fifteen he applied for admission to South High School. The principal tried to dissuade him, telling him that the students were rough and thoughtless and would probably crowd him into a fall on the stairways. He pointed out many valid reasons why Edward should not enroll. Edward said quietly, "I'll take my chances, as I've always done. A fall or two more won't hurt me. I'm coming anyway."

Kuncel was enrolled, and history was made. He earned a straight "A" average in each of his subjects, a scholastic record never made before or since by any student in that school. He was class valedictorian. But he had only started. He enrolled in Creighton University in Omaha, working his way by heavy physical work. He loaded and unloaded trucks, working by the sense of touch and hearing. He suffered physical hurts from time to time, but his spirit was unhurtable. Physical obstacles aplenty, but never any sense of frustration. His scholastic record again stood out. He was graduated summa cum laude and Phi Beta Kappa.

Edward applied for a vacant position teaching in South High. His teaching record is as outstanding as his student record. His classes are full; his students respect him and they love his cheery, optimistic approach to life. He did graduate work at Creighton while teaching at South High, received his Master's degree and ultimately his Ph.D. His wife and small son think there is no one like Daddy. Edward Kuncel might easily have decided that life's cards were stacked against him and feebly surrendered. He has proved that obstacles are not the cause of frustration, for obstacles, like beauty, lie only in the mind of the beholder.

OUTSTANDING AMERICAN MOTHER

One more illustration. Each year a mothers' committee in each of the United States selects one or two outstanding women and sends their names in to a central committee. From among this group one only is ultimately selected as the "American Mother." In 1946, Mrs. Emma Clement was selected. Her genealogical line runs clear back into the heart of Africa, for both her parents were slaves on a plantation. Emma's parents came north following the Civil War, poor but hopeful of a fighting chance at life. Emma had learned how to do without things; so, when she was accepted as a college student, she didn't mind having to do without things which other girls had; her mind was on the delightful thought that she would be equipped for the teaching profession. On her graduation day she married a young student going into the ministry. They had eight children, went through the agony of losing one, and dedicated each of the others to God. Through storm and sunshine, this family struggled along on the meager salary of a country minister, often paid in the form of chickens or potatoes. Mrs. Clement lost her husband but determined that these children she had dedicated to God should be given to Him well trained, at any cost to her.

Now, let us look at them. One son is president of Atlanta University. Another is pastor of the African M. E. Zion Church in Cambridge, Massachusetts. Another is with the American Red Cross, and another is Professor of Physics at West Virginia State College. One daughter is Professor of English at Tuskegee, another is in the Department of English at Kentucky State College, while the third is Executive Secretary of the Missionary Society of the A.M.E. Church. Seven shining jewels in the crown of the daughter of a slave. A family as distinguished as any in the entire history of the United States. Emma Clement has every right to be called the American Mother of 1946 or of any year.

Mrs. Clement does not talk about it, but unquestionably this family has had its humiliating moments. Prejudice and discrimination have certainly leveled their poisoned shafts at its members many times. Their racial origin has undoubtedly blocked them from certain greatly desired goals. They could quite easily have become bitter, soured, hated, and hating. They could have thrown in the sponge and said, "What's the use?" as others have done. They could have turned to Communism, thinking they would attain to an equality denied them under the American system. But they were able to see life whole, not in its little vicious parts. No member of this outstanding family is rich with this world's goods, but they are rich in those things that make for rich living. They can face life head-on, take whatever life throws at them, and can turn aside what they do not want while accepting that which they want. And after all, this is all there is to living— heart serene, a courage high, ideals maintained, standards met, and goals attained.

WHERE FRUSTRATION REALLY LIES

What, then, is frustration? Where does it start and wherein does it lie? If deafness, blindness, lameness, illness, poverty, or racial discrimination causes it in some, while others in identical situations rise above it, it must lie in one's inner attitudes. Yes, but which attitudes? If we can discover what it is in each instance, we shall have the answer to this ugly problem of frustration.

We can leave the question of whether one is born either determined or spineless, for if we grant this premise, there would be no incentive for striving. If one is born to be defeated, why should he make any effort to achieve something for which he has not the equipment? We can also leave the question of one's early conditioning, since this essay is directed toward those of adult years who want to know how to overcome already developed feelings of frustration. To admit that our character is unchangeably set because we were started wrongly is just about as fatalistic as the belief that we were born quitters. We can also blot out the belief that one is frustrated just because he has not been able to attain a certain goal, whether it be riches, fame, or marriage. Millions who never attained any of these have lived lives completely free of any sense of frustration.

THE ANSWER TO FRUSTRATION

THE QUESTION OF to be or not to be frustrated is basically one of our reaction to life. Our reaction to life depends on what we believe to be our resources. Our resources depend on our concept of power. This is the crux of the problem. It is a question of relative power, the power opposing and the power with which to meet this obstruction.

Assuming that two members of a family have grown up under the same set of influences but with opposite results, their concept of relative power must have been the determining influence. The obstacles in each case were identical in their menacing quality; therefore the power available to each must have been differently seen and grasped. A good general knows that he can win every battle if he is able to throw his greatest power at the point of his enemy's weakest power. A football coach tries to throw his greatest power at the weakest point in his opponent's line. A boxer or tennis player keeps concentrating on his opponent's weaker side. In each instance the weakness of our opponent makes us seem stronger than he; we gain a consciousness of greater power.

There is such a thing as the habit of success. The awareness of power grows with use. Jack Dempsey was discouraged and ready to quit boxing after several tough matches with little money. Jack Kearns came along and kept building Dempsey up mentally. In one sense it can be said that Dempsey learned courage. He was made aware of the fact that he possessed greater power than other men in his profession. Even when Dempsey lost, Kearns showed him wherein he had failed to apply his greatest power and encouraged him not to make the same mistakes again. By a shrewd revelation of Dempsey's greater relative power, he brought him to the world's championship.

DEVELOPING THE CONSCIOUSNESS OF POWER

IN THE MATTER OF physical prowess, it is comparatively easy to develop this consciousness of physical power. In things mental and spiritual it is more difficult. But it can be done. Every person who has ever attained emotional maturity has done it, either consciously or unconsciously, through the cultivation of this sense of superior power. They saw the difficulties, they knew these difficulties had stopped others, but they said, "I can handle this." They were not bluffing, nor were they kidding themselves. The bluffer can be stopped, and is stopped sooner or later. But he who actually believes within himself that he has sufficient power can never be stopped.

This leads us to say that each of us has within himself sufficient force to take him over any obstruction that lies across his path. There is nothing anywhere in the universe that can permanently block Life from surging outward into complete expression except the person's own belief to the contrary. This is the only barrier to fullest expression, for "It is done unto us as we believe."

The next question is, "Is this power a natural endowment or something to which we attach ourselves?" It is both. It can best be illustrated by a story which has inspired men for almost three thousand years.

AN OLD STORY WITH AN INNER MEANING

IN THE STORY OF David and Goliath there is a very subtle message hidden away. As we have often pointed out, the Bible has a primary and a secondary interpretation. On the surface it is a history of the Jews and of the early Christian church. On the hidden side it is a history of man. It is a psychological drama of the conflict between man's higher and his lower nature. Man is defeated when he works only with his external, obvious powers; he wins when he finds access to his secret, hidden forces. Skillfully interwoven into the historical records of the doings of the children of Israel is a deeper spiritual story which is ageless. The superficial reader gets the surface story and often finds contradictions which make him reject the Book. The intuitive reader sees the scarlet thread running just beneath the surface which makes the Book a priceless revelation of man's actual and potential inner power. The ancients loved to hide their teaching from superficial eyes, leaving it for those who could penetrate beneath the surface and read the language of the heart.

David and Goliath is a story of frustration and of the resources available for its overcoming. This particular event may have been an actual historical battle or it may be folklore. It may have been written up and inserted in this part of the history of Israel as a fitting place in which to insert a spiritual lesson. Its historical accuracy is not important—its lesson is.

SPIRITUAL VS. MATERIAL FORCE

David was the youngest of the sons of Jesse. Whenever a second son or the youngest son is mentioned in these Bible narratives, one reads more closely, because the younger son always refers to man's spiritual nature. Man is born a physical son first; he lives in his physical nature in a physical world, eating physical food and begetting physical children. But his advanced or spiritual nature is to emerge later, living in a spiritual world, nourished on spiritual food, and begetting spiritual children, which are his ideas, ideals, concepts, and thoughts pertaining to that great spiritual world with which we are constantly surrounded.

Goliath represents brute force—sheer, unspiritual, earthly. He is of the Philistines, who always represent the unspiritual world. Day after day, he walked on the mountainside in front of the Philistines and hurled his challenge across the valley to the Israelites. "Send out your champion and let us fight. If I win, you will be our slaves. If your man wins, we shall become your slaves." He was huge, menacing, supposed to be over eleven feet tall. His spear was too heavy for any other man to use. He was unbeatable, or appeared to be. He represents that great unbeatable problem of illness or poverty or the destructive habit which challenges our manhood, but which it seems impossible to conquer.

David's older brothers were in the army, and Jesse sent David with bread and cheese for them, he being just a stripling at the time. He was shocked that no one accepted the Philistine's challenge. His brothers cowered in fear and shrank away from Goliath. They represent natural man, weighing material force against material menace, and feeling that they are not strong enough to win. The result, frustration.

David, being the youngest son, represents spiritual force.

Unawed by Goliath's physical appearance, unafraid of his terrifying strength and power, he accepted the challenge. Spiritual power can always defeat earthly force. His brothers tried to dissuade him, for they had only one standard of measurement, the physical. The earth-minded person can never appreciate spiritual power, because he is unacquainted with it. They tried to persuade David to put on armor. He consented but then rejected it—it would only hamper him—spiritual power is not augmented by material armor.

THE ETERNAL SPIRITUAL LAW

GOLIATH WAS INSULTED by this stripling's acceptance of his challenge and told him that he would feed his body to the buzzards. David replied, "Thou comest to me with a sword and shield, but I come to thee in the name of the Lord of Hosts." The word "Lord" in the Bible can always be interchanged with the expression "spiritual law." The ancients knew the secrets of spiritual law. Moses, the Prophets, and Daniel had all worked seeming miracles through spiritual law. This Creative Law had brought the world into being, was maintaining it in space, breathing life into every child after it had carefully and skillfully built it in the womb. It had healed lepers and done many marvelous things, of which their history was filled. David was coming in the name of this Creative Law, with a slingshot against sword and shield, yet certain of victory. It is the age-old ascendancy of things unseen over things seen, of mind over matter.

There are many interpretive details concerning the stones, sling, and equipment, for which there is not space here. But whoever heard of slingshot against sword and shield? It was ridiculous, asinine!

As the story goes, David threw one small, smooth stone. It hit the giant in the middle of his forehead and he went down. David rushed over and cut off his head, and it was all over.

WHERE THE POWER LIES

We might say that David's skill with the sling was a cultivated asset and his throwing coordination an inherent ability, so that man uses inherent powers in meeting his menaces. But in reality it was not the stone which put the giant down. It was David's sense of power on his side, the power of the Creative Law. He and his brothers both were confronted by the obstacle of Goliath. They shrank back while he went eagerly forward. Their different reactions were the result of their view of life, or, shall we say, their awareness of the immensity of the power available.

David never once said, "I'll kill him with this slingshot." His faith was in "the name of the Law." A son bears his father's name and presumably his character. David saw himself as having the same character as the Creative Law which knows nothing of any hostile opposing power. It is conscious only of its ability to do. David was enlisting this undefeatable Law on his side and really and fully believed that it was working through him. The greatest man in the army of Israel that day was puny compared to this giant who opposed them, but this giant was puny compared to the Creative Law. David was taking on the character along with the name of the Law, thereby magnifying himself beyond measure.

MAN'S INCREASING AWARENESS OF POWER

PRESENT-DAY MAN is so recently disconnected from his animal ancestry that the talk of higher spiritual force is sometimes foolishness to him. In geological time man has been on the earth less than a minute compared to the life strain from which he has sprung. His few thousand years of recorded history are less than one second of geologic time. Naturally, he is proud of his advanced knowledge of earth, stars, and atom. But it is his attachment on the physical side that has caused him to delve so deeply into inventions which add only to his creature comfort or safety. He has not yet scratched the surface of that vast realm of intuitive knowledge which still lies largely hidden from sight; yet there are hints and evidences of this spiritual world, governed by laws as exact as those of the sciences. He is delving somewhat gingerly into psychology, which is a study of the laws of thought.

Beyond this psychological area lies another, more finely attenuated than even the mental. True, it is contacted by mental means; yet strangely enough it seems to flow into action when one allows the wheels of his mind to run down. By this we certainly do not mean that it is contacted through any self-hypnotic trance. Perhaps the better word is silence. One brings himself into a state of inner silence, in a state of what has been called meditation. The Quaker George Fox said that God is always speaking to man but that we are so busy chattering that we don't hear Him. Only when we become silent with a deep inner silence do we hear God.

But the world is too busy for this and dismisses it as so much nonsense. Perhaps the weird hallucinations that some unbalanced persons have reported in this direction have given the world cause for scorn. Yet history carries many instances of sane, well-balanced men and women who have experienced the reality of Something contacted only through this inner silence. They have been chiefly, although not always, church people, to whom meditation and inner silence were habitual.

THE POWER AVAILABLE

The chief value of all this to us is that there are powers available to man which far transcend those which the average man is using. Their names do not matter so much as their existence does. When Charles Steinmetz was asked what he thought the great discovery of the coming century would be, he astonished his questioner by not mentioning anything in his specialty, the field of electricity. He said that the next great discovery would be of a set of vibrations governed by exact laws but of a distinctly spiritual nature. He asserted that these rays play constantly upon man and have great healing power. Whether they come from outer space or are inherent in all space was not made clear.

The whole Science of Mind philosophy is based upon the existence of such laws. We go on the assumption that there is an Infinite Healing Presence in the Universe and in man, for otherwise no healing, medical or spiritual, could take place. And this Presence, or Law, or Principle, or whatever men choose to call it, seems to be immediately available to man when its conditions have been met. Just as electricity needs tight connections in order to flow, and an aeroplane needs sufficient lift and drive in order to fly, so this spiritual Law seems to operate in the heart opened to kindliness, honesty of purpose, and sincere goodwill. It can be stopped by fear, hate, anxiety. Why this is we do not know. To later researchers our efforts may appear childish and elementary; yet in the short distance this generation has been able to go, this unnamable Presence seems to have cooperated in astounding healings which have had medical authorities puzzled.

In our private classes, we sometimes say, "When the knowledge of the power outweighs the fear of the condition, the person can be healed. So long as the fear of the condition outweighs the assurance of the Power, he cannot be healed." Perhaps this is the key to the flow of this spiritual force. Whether the term "God," "Nature," "Infinite Intelligence," "Mind," or "Rays" is used is not important. The chief thing for the good of mankind is that the Source be contacted. Man contacted gravity and electricity long before he named them.

THE CURE FOR FRUSTRATION

THE CURE FOR frustration lies in thus contacting Power. A problem looms large or small according to the power available to meet it. He who remains ignorant of spiritual power is then dwarfed by his problems. He who becomes conversant with spiritual power dwarfs his problems. It is as simple as that. How it is done, or why, might not be answered yet. Later centuries might unravel it. But this Power is available right now to the least among us, as thousands of men and women are discovering.

It has been estimated that fifteen million men and women in the United States are using this power in healing today, partially or totally. Men are cooperating with it for the solution of business problems and for the increasing of their business volume. We said earlier that Life seems to have an impulse to thrust outward through us, to enlarge itself through living channels. Might we not find eventually that Life is personal rather than impersonal? Might it not be that Life is what we now call God? Some of those whom we mentioned earlier as having flown in the face of their physical and other obstructions, risen above them, and attained the heights were not members of the regularly constituted church. Their theological position was by no means orthodox; yet this Power seemed quite ready to flow through them, enabling them to surmount their problems. This Power is one which seems to focus itself in attitudes rather than in creeds. This makes it something that can be used universally, by all men, of any belief, in any land. It cuts across national and theological boundaries yet does not call upon anyone either to forsake or to join a church.

LINKING ONESELF WITH THE POWER

The flow of this Power is based upon a certain concept. One flees into frustration or advances into liberty by his grasp of this concept, which is that whatever is true of this Power becomes true of him who links himself up with It. Since It is greater than anything that can ever come up against It, so man is greater than anything he ever comes up against. He is not necessarily smarter or stronger than others, as an individual, but he allows Something irresistible to occupy him and to operate within him.

One of the most significant statements ever made is, "I and the Father are One." This is what David was thinking as he approached Goliath. The Infinite Power is also the Infinite Intelligence. Man's mind is part of this Infinite Mind. So long as he fails to see or refuses to admit this, he is just one man walking his lonely path through life. The moment he comes to a clear grasp of it, he walks no longer alone. He and the Father walk together through life. The Father's Power becomes his Power. Man provides the proper type of attitude; the Father provides the dynamic. Someone has said, "One with God is a majority." It becomes an unbeatable majority when approached from this point of view, with all the Father's resources at man's disposal.

THE ANSWER TO EVERY PROBLEM

PSYCHOLOGISTS ARE SOMETIMES amazed at the almost unfathomable depths of the human mind. Man's mind is not a shallow pool; it is as deep as eternity. Because it is the Infinite Mind flowing through him, it contains the answer to every problem. Our surface mind is so occupied with daily affairs that those eternal answers hidden far in the depths do not often rise to the surface. But one can cultivate a mode of thought which allows more and more to float up. This streaming Infinite Mind flowing through man as his mind contains all knowledge of past, present, and future. It contains the knowledge of how every successful plan was ever carried out; it knows how new cells are built. Better still, it seems to be quite willing to yield up this or any knowledge which is for the expansion of man's good. There is no reluctance or holding back on its part. The blockage is all on our side, in that we do not dare to claim big things from it.

In his present stage of development, man is like a child standing on the shore of a limitless ocean. He knows that it is there, but he does not dare launch himself on it. Even the heights reached by the loftiest souls are still those of the child on the seashore. One spiritually minded logician, the Apostle Paul, hinted at this vast unexplored area when he said, "Eye hath not seen, nor ear heard, neither have entered into the heart of man the things which God hath prepared for them that love Him." Granted that this is a somewhat archaic way of stating this truth, it still remains that the theologian Paul and the scientist Steinmetz were saying the same thing. Undoubtedly, man will advance his knowledge in this field. Generation after generation will venture further into this limitless ocean, until man will not only solve his personal problems but will learn how to dissolve national and international feelings of frustration until war itself will become only a historical memory of man's barbaric days of partial vision.